"For 20 years I have benefited from the creative f
Dr. Charles Arn. His new book *How to Start a New Ser*
methods—based on excellent research—for lay a
people."

Raymond W. Hurn, Church of the Nazarene, General Superintendent, Emeritus

"Charles Arn has done wonderful research of a very valuable approach to reaching the unchurched. This very practicable and understandable book should be read by pastors, church planters, and congregational leaders. In fifty years in ministry and supervision, I have not seen a resource that I would recommend more highly."

Clarence A. Kopp, Church of the United Brethren in Christ, Bishop Emeritus

"Half of the congregations in North America need to expand their weekend worship services. Read this book and you will learn how to do it successfully."

Lyle Schaller, Author, Parish Consultant

"This is a timely book that gives insight by a leading church growth consultant to help pastors and lay readers maximize church facilities and ministries for outreach and growth. *How to Start a New Service* is the best book I have read on how to start new worship services in the local church."

Ray W. Ellis, Free Methodist Church of North America, Director of Evangelism

"I get more questions from pastors and planning committees on multiple worship services than any other subject. Now there's a primary source that I can recommend. Even if you are only beginning to think about adding a worship service to your weekend schedule, get this book. It will steer you into the right direction and help you make good decisions. And if you have reached near capacity on Sunday morning, or want to reach a new group of people, or start a new church, this book will give you a wealth of information and choices."

Dirk J. Hart, Christian Reformed Church of North America,
Minister of Evangelism

"*How to Start a New Service* is loaded with insights for any pastor with a heart for reaching others. Charles Arn is one of the most insightful thinkers in the church growth field today. Of course, I may be somewhat prejudiced!"

Win Arn, Author, Producer

"It's a good book. Exciting. I kept asking myself 'What if this really works?' Imagine thousands of churches across America following Charles' prescription. It would be wonderful."

Leith Anderson, Senior Pastor, Wooddale Church

"*How to Start a New Service* demonstrates why Charles Arn is a leading spokesperson for the Church Growth Movement. Destined to be a classic, this strategic book presents both the 'why's' and 'how's' of adding new style worship services which will reach new people for Christ. Do you desire to see an increase in your total worship attendance? Then buy, read, and use this book."

Gary L. McIntosh, Professor of Christian Ministry and Leadership,
Talbot School of Theology

"'Should our church start a new service?' is a critical question for thousands of church leaders today. Charles Arn's national research gives clear, practical answers. Here's what you need to know before you grow."

Kevin A. Miller, Editor, Leadership Journal

"Charles Arn provides a much needed book for the church on a timely topic that continues to stir controversy. *How to Start a New Service* is not a philosophical dissertation on what might work. It is a practical tool, based on documented research, which shares strategic plans and tested procedures that lead to the implementation of a new form of worship. This book should become a much used resource in the library of every pastor and church leader that seeks to relate the Gospel of Jesus Christ to an ever changing world."

Kenneth W. Behnkin, Lutheran Church—Missouri Synod, Missions and Evangelism, Pacific Southwest District

"This book provides all the information any pastor would need to add a new church service. It is thorough and complete."

Charles Hackett, Assemblies of God, Division of Home Missions

"Dr. Charles Arn uses a balanced approach to the subject. His thoroughly researched conclusions about adding a new service will help any leader considering the idea. This book is a 'must' read on the subject."

Marlin Mull, The Wesleyan Church, General Director of Evangelism and Church Growth

"This book tells you anything you ever wanted to know about how to start a new service. Charles Arn leaves 'no stone unturned.' Pastors shouldn't even think about starting a new service until they have read this book."

Bill M. Sullivan, Church of the Nazarene, Church Growth Division Director

"Charles Arn's book *How to Start a New Service* is a tremendous motivator. It is the most comprehensive publication that I have read on the subject. I sincerely believe God will use this practical book to resurrect many churches in America that have reached a plateau."

Bill Sheeks, Church of God, Cleveland, Tennessee, General Secretary

"Well researched, biblically sound, practical—must reading for anyone interested in reaching more people for Christ and his church. This book is not only a must for those considering addition of a 'new service' but for those who have a passion for communicating the gospel effectively to modern society."

Jack Barker, Cumberland Presbyterian Church, Executive Director, Board of Missions

"Simple says it best. One can toss a 'flurry' of church growth tactics to a congregation and create a fog or provide a well-focused formula and create a clear, productive path. Charles Arn teaches us that working smarter is better than working harder. Creating new worship services is clearly working smarter."

Paul Mundey, Senior Pastor, Frederick Church of the Brethren, Frederick, MD

"Pastors, worship leaders, and lay leaders alike will find this book informative and helpful. It is a road map to better understand the dynamics of change within a congregation, the issues surrounding the development of an additional worship service, and the spark that can lead a church to new growth."

Stephen Wagner, Senior Pastor, Prince of Peace Lutheran Church, Carrollton, TX

"For churches experiencing 'bad news' in church growth, this book is powerful 'good news.' Dr. Arn relects a deep-seated optimism that God's people can be renewed and start a new thing."

Charles R. Shumate, Church Growth Ministries, Church of God, Anderson, IN

How to Start a New Service

Other Books by Charles Arn with Win Arn
Catch the Age Wave
Growth: A New Vision for the Sunday School
Live Long and Love It
The Master's Plan for Making Disciples
Who Cares about Love?

How to Start a New Service

Your Church Can Reach New People

Charles Arn

Foreword by Leith Anderson

Baker Books

A Division of Baker Book House Co
Grand Rapids, Michigan 49516

Published by Baker Books
a division of Baker Book House Company
P.O. Box 6287, Grand Rapids, MI 49516-6287

Seventh printing, December 2004

Printed in the Unites States of America

Library of Congress Cataloging-in-Publication Data
Arn, Charles.
    How to start a new service : your church can reach new people / Charles Arn.
        p. cm.
    Includes bibliographical references.
    ISBN 0-8010-9037-7 (pbk.)
    1. Public worship. 2. Church growth. I. Title.
BV15.A76 1997
264—dc21   97-1377

For current information about all releases from Baker Book House, visit our web site:
http://www.bakerbooks.com

To the two most influential people in my life,
Barbara and Win Arn—my mom and dad.
Thank you for the countless wonderful times
we have shared together.

And to my new wife, Ann, as we begin
our journey in life together.

Contents

List of Figures

Foreword

Matthew, Mark, Luke, and John compose the four Gospels of Jesus Christ. Wouldn't you think that one would have been enough? The first three say pretty much the same thing; the fourth is very different. Approximately 95 percent of the Gospel of Mark appears almost word-for-word in the Gospel of Matthew.

Why four? Certainly God could have limited himself to a single Gospel to tell the story of Jesus, but he recognized that different groups of people receive the good news in different ways. Matthew is written to a Jewish audience with many references to the Old Testament and to Hebrew culture. Mark is the short Gospel, written to a Gentile audience which had little knowledge or understanding of Jewish religion. Each group got its own Gospel so that the message could be clearly understood.

If we choose to follow God's New Testament pattern, we will provide different channels to effectively communicate the good news today. We aren't writing new Gospels, but we can have new church services.

Consider the advantages of a movement to start new church services:

1. *Restored emphasis on God*. Single services done in traditional ways can confuse tradition with God. But when a new service is started, a church must set aside tradition and carefully consider core beliefs about God, the central importance of Jesus Christ, and the different ways God can be worshiped. This is not unlike the challenge facing a missionary who takes

the gospel of Jesus Christ into a different culture: clearly defining what is eternal and what is changeable.

2. *More people reached for Jesus Christ.* The number of people attending two services will almost always be more than the number of people attending one service. Even if the increase were only 10 percent, the potential across North America would be to reach millions more. Imagine the potential of one hundred thousand churches adding an additional church service to their weekly schedules.

3. *Financial efficiency.* New church services cost hundreds or thousands of dollars. New church buildings cost hundreds of thousands or millions of dollars. When congregations choose more services instead of more new auditoriums, millions more dollars are available to invest in mission and ministry. This is particularly important at a time when fewer churches have the resources for construction and when many churches don't have enough land to expand.

Sometimes I am asked, "Which Wooddale Church worship service do you like best?" My answer is quick and honest, "That's like asking a parent, 'Which of your children do you love the most?'" Parents know that every child is different but every child is loved. Each child has definite likes and dislikes, definite strengths and abilities. No parent requires every child to be exactly alike—that's not fair and it wouldn't work anyway. Well, just as our children at home are different, so the people the church seeks to reach are different. Love them equally but reach them differently.

Leith Anderson
Wooddale Church
Eden Prairie, Minnesota

11

Acknowledgments

Thank you to the churches that participated in this pioneering study of new services and church growth: Conservative Baptist Church (Pacific Northwest), Evangelical Lutheran Church in America (Northeast Ohio Synod), United Presbyterian Church USA (Memphis and Redstone Presbyteries), Salvation Army (Northwest and Intermountain Divisions), Lutheran Church—Missouri Synod (Southeast District), and the churches that participated in the interdenominational New Beginnings projects in Los Angeles and Chicago. Your risktaking and pioneering work will benefit many other churches throughout North America and see many new people become part of the Christian community of faith.

Introduction

Vineyard Community Church in Cincinnati, Ohio, has grown in fifteen years from six couples meeting in a living room to a congregation of three thousand people attending seven weekly worship services in a six-hundred-seat auditorium. Despite the fact that it has planted twelve daughter churches, it continues to grow with 20 percent of its new members being recent converts. "I'm seriously praying about going to an eighth service," says founding pastor Steve Sjogren, "because it would make room for more seekers. Even though that's what we said about the fourth, fifth, sixth, and seventh services, I still can't find any biblical reason to stop."

Westminster Presbyterian Church in Duluth, Minnesota, was a declining church in an aging community. By 1992 worship attendance averaged forty people per Sunday, and the church had not reached anyone for Christ in over five years. "They wanted to grow but didn't know how," says Rev. Chuck Laird, who was called as pastor in 1993. Two years later Westminster added a new worship service to reach Baby Boomers. At this writing the church is averaging over two hundred people per Sunday in combined attendance—the highest in its thirty-three-year history. "Through the new service we are reaching people we simply could not have reached any other way," says Laird. "I believe God would have this church approaching one thousand within five years. But it will never happen with only two services."

Prince of Peace Lutheran Church in Carrollton, Texas, begins its Sunday like most other Lutheran churches—with a traditional, liturgical worship service. By the end of the week, however, the church has conducted three more services, each distinct in focus and style, that attract people who are entirely different from traditional Lutherans. "Each time we added a worship hour," says Rev. Steve Wagner, "our attendance increased by 20 percent. I am amazed at the power of the worship style to define the character of the congregation attending. Offering distinct choices simply allows more people to identify with our church and hear our message—the gospel of Jesus Christ."

These churches represent thousands of congregations across America. In every denomination and in every part of the country, church leaders are wondering about a new type of service. New phrases are entering our vocabulary: alternative service, contemporary service, Saturday night service, seeker-sensitive service, seeker-targeted service, or simply second (or third, or eighth) service. Church leaders are asking themselves, "Should we add a new service? If so, when? And how?" (Throughout this book the phrase "new service" should be interpreted to mean "new *style* service," as distinguished from another, identical service.)

Approximately half of the 355,000 Protestant churches in the United States and Canada should consider adding a new service to their weekly schedule of activities. Of the churches that add a new service, eight out of ten will experience a measurable increase in (1) total worship attendance, (2) total giving, and (3) total number of Christian conversions.

My study of the dynamics of adding a new worship service and how doing so would subsequently affect church growth started with a five-year research project with Church Growth, Inc. (Monrovia, Calif.). During this time we (1) researched established churches that have attempted—successfully or unsuccessfully—to add a new service, (2) identified common denominators of the successful models, and (3) worked with several hundred volunteer churches of different sizes, locations, and denominations to test the steps of adding a new service. The result of this research is a considerable body of knowledge and experience that can help other churches successfully begin a new service.

Churches That Should Not Add a New Service

So how can you determine if your church is one of the approx-imately 177,500 churches that should be planning a new service in the coming year? It is actually easier to tell whether you are *not* one of those churches. Below are four situations which describe approximately half the churches in North America. If you find that your church is in one of these situations, I believe you would do well to focus on strategies of church growth other than adding a new service:

1. Do not add a new service if community is the highest priority of your church. The most frequent comments you will hear if you now have one worship service and begin planning a second are: "We won't know each other" and "We will become two churches."

Do you know what? They're right!

Churches that add a new style service to their weekly program find that attenders gravitate toward one of the services, infre-quently interacting with those in the other service (or services). Churches that decide to move ahead with a new service must con-clude that "becoming two churches" is not necessarily bad.

If your leaders and/or members, however, are primarily com-mitted to preserving "one happy family," an attempt to begin a new service will be frustrating and will probably fail. The new ser-vice will be perceived as counterproductive to congregational com-munity and will be stonewalled by those who see it as a threat to such community. A pastor who continues to pursue a new service in a church determined to preserve community will soon be look-ing for another church. (This may not necessarily be bad if the pastor believes that Christ's church is called to a higher purpose than preserving community.)

2. Do not add a new service if preserving tradition is the highest priority of your church. Congregations and denominations that have split from a more liberal church or denomination in the past fifty to seventy-five years often have greater difficulty adding a new service. Even churches that do not have such a background but emphasize correct doctrine and interpretation of Scripture as their distinctive encounter difficulty adding a new style service. "Con-

15

temporary" is seen as compromise. "Contemporary Christian music" is considered an oxymoron. A true church, these good-hearted souls believe, could not possibly look so much like the world. In fact, the greater the difference between the church and the world, the purer and more preserved the doctrine and faith is seen to be.

If such an attitude permeates your membership, a new service will cause a church split! Supporters of the "worldly" service will be seen as agents of disruption bringing the carnality of the world inside the walls of the church. Of course, those observations are accurate to a certain extent. A new service very well may bring the world inside the walls of the church. To some that is the greatest of successes, for it is what Christ calls the church to do. But to others it is the greatest of sins.

3. Do not add a new service if survival is the highest priority of your church. Every year three thousand to five thousand churches close their doors for the last time. Most of these churches spent great time and effort in the years preceding that final day trying to avoid such a fate. Many other churches are in the final years of their life. Their attention, energy, pastoral focus, and member recruitment are intended to simply keep the doors open.

Preoccupation with avoiding death creates a self-fulfilling prophecy. Such churches invariably die, if not through formal dis-solution, then through a degenerative slide into spiritual impo-tence. Just as a human body may appear to be alive despite the absence of brain activity, a church may appear to be alive despite the absence of a vision for the future. But neither is really alive. And both will die. If your church is more concerned with avoid-ing death than pursuing life, a new service will fail.

4. Do not add a new service if the senior pastor intends to leave in the coming year. The senior pastor is one of the most important factors in the success of adding a new service. I have found that if all else is equal, when the pastor is actively supporting a new ser-vice the chances of success are approximately 80 percent. With-out his or her support, the chances drop to under 20 percent. But when the pastor leaves in the midst of such planning, the likeli-hood of a successful new service drops to under 5 percent.

Research studies have shown that the departure of a pastor is counterproductive for most congregations.[1] A pastor's exit in the midst of any major initiative, including adding a new service, has the same effect as a general deserting his troops in the height of battle. No pastor should leave such a situation with a clear conscience.

Based on my experience, research, and involvement in the church growth movement during the past twenty-one years, I believe it is fair to suggest that approximately 50 percent of the congregations in North America fall into one of the above categories. (My assessment is that approximately 15 percent of all churches fall into the first category, 10 percent fall into the second, 5 percent into the third, and 20 percent into the fourth.) If your church is in one or more of these four categories, your needs are most likely beyond the scope of this book. There are strategies and resources that can help. But starting a new service is probably not one of them.[2]

However, if you are among the 50 percent who do not fall into one of these categories, your time may be at hand! I believe your church has a great opportunity to broaden the scope and impact of its ministry—and the kingdom of God—in your community! You should begin planning a new service.

Good Excuses but Not Good Reasons

Some readers may be saying, "Yes, but my situation is different. I'm not sure we can start a new service because . . ." Indeed, you may have a legitimate reason for not planning a new service in the coming year. But based on my research and experience, none of the following qualify as legitimate reasons:

1. We're not big enough to begin a new service. I have found that the minimum number of people needed in your present service to begin a new service is approximately fifty. If you have less than fifty people in attendance (and have had for the past three years), I suggest you follow the guidelines in this book but apply them to your one existing service. That is, start a new service but put

17

your old service out of its misery! If you have fifty people or more in your present service, you have enough to begin a new service.

2. *We're not growing.* The growth pattern of your existing service (or services) is basically irrelevant to starting a new service. In fact, if there is any relationship at all, it is inverse: The more rapidly you are declining, the more immediately you should move to begin a new service. Doing more of what you're doing will get you more of what you're getting. The sooner you begin planning a new service, the more quickly you can expect things to turn around.

3. *Our sanctuary isn't full in the present service(s).* The thinking process of some well-meaning people is: "Our present service(s) isn't full. If people wanted to come to our church, they could attend the one(s) we have." As we will see later in the book, this assumption is quite mistaken. At the same time, however, there is a relationship between your sanctuary capacity, your attendance levels, and a new service:

- If attendance at your present service averages less than 20 percent of sanctuary capacity (and has for the past two or more years), you need a new service as soon as possible. The chances of your present service growing are minimal, and the new service is your primary hope for survival.
- If your attendance averages 20 to 40 percent of sanctuary capacity, a new service still has a better chance to grow than your existing one(s).
- If attendance averages 40 to 60 percent of sanctuary capacity, a new service will not significantly reduce the growth potential of your present service(s).
- If your sanctuary is at 60 to 80 percent of capacity, you face a challenging situation. There is a good chance that your new service will, in fact, take enough people away from your present service to drop it into the 40 to 60 percent range, a capacity rating less conducive for growth. The key question in this case is whether your attendance has been growing during the past two years. If attendance has been growing (10 percent or more per year), I suggest you set a date one to one and a

18

half years away for adding a new service and allow your present growth pattern to continue. If your attendance has been stagnant for the past two or more years, you should begin planning for a new service if you want your total attendance to grow. If you don't, it won't.

- If your present service regularly fills your sanctuary to 80 percent or more of capacity, I suggest that you immediately add another identical service. The saturation point of most facilities (including your parking lot, by the way) is reached when it averages 80 to 85 percent of total capacity for more than four months. If, for example, your sanctuary holds 300 people and you are averaging 250, you are full and won't grow beyond your present size.

Figure 1 illustrates the likelihood of a new service negatively influencing the growth potential of your present service(s) as a function of sanctuary capacity (assuming the style and time of your existing service(s) do not change).

Figure 1

Likelihood of New Service Negatively Affecting Existing Service(s)

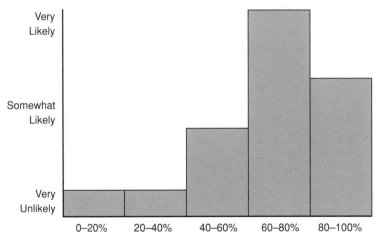

19

This graph represents good news and bad news. The bad news is that present attendance in many churches is in the 60 to 80 percent range of sanctuary capacity—the point at which a new service is most likely to negatively affect the growth of the existing service(s). The good news is that for churches at this stage, a new service will add to total attendance, whereas otherwise growth would stop once 80 percent of capacity was reached.

When you calculate your sanctuary capacity, by the way, don't use figures from when the building was constructed. If your church has pews, your capacity has declined if your building was constructed over twenty years ago, even if the number of pews has not changed! Architects and church planners used to calculate that an eight-foot pew would seat five people. Today that same pew will comfortably seat three. A generation ago people were comfortable with twenty inches of space. Today the comfort zone is thirty to thirty-six inches.[3]

4. We don't have enough personnel. A new service will indeed require more people. A contemporary service, for example, requires three to four times the amount of preparation that worship planners generally spend on a traditional service(s). But staffing a new service requires fewer human resources than one might imagine and usually less than a traditional service with a choir. "I propose that the missing ingredient in developing multiple worship services is . . . the lack of vision in how to raise enough lay talent to staff the additional services," notes Carl George.[4] I have found that when it comes to adding a new service, lack of pastoral willingness to reallocate time is a greater obstacle than lack of people.

5. Our theology does not allow for a different style. I was recently discouraged by a conversation with an Episcopal priest on the topic of new style services. We were discussing the difference between form and essence of worship. He surprised me with a statement about many churches in his denomination by saying, "For us, our form *is* our essence." How sad.

It is critical to struggle with the difference between your form and your essence, your style and your substance, your negotiables and your nonnegotiables. We can observe religious groups in our own country's history who have allowed their forms to become their essence. The Shakers, for example, are nearly extinct because of their uncompromising religious rituals; the Amish, who survive only on biological growth, are losing many of their youth.

Our convictions of God's truth can and must be timeless. But the forms through which those convictions are demonstrated to those unlike us must be able to change. Such struggles with form and essence are not new to the Christian church. The Jewish Christians faced the same soul-searching issues when the gospel jumped the culture barrier to the Samaritans. But it is a struggle that must be waged regularly for the church—for your church—to preach a relevant Christ.

6. Our church is in a bad location. Research has shown that location is not a predictor of church growth. A good location does not cause growth; a bad location seldom prohibits growth. Some of the most rapidly growing churches are in economically depressed areas, or locations that require a diligent search to find them.

Certainly there are some churches that are in the wrong place. Approximately 10 percent of all congregations, according to Lyle Schaller, will not grow in their present location.[5] In many such cases the makeup of the neighborhood changed while the congregation did not. But in actuality it is these churches, more than most, that should begin immediate plans for a new service. A new style service targeted for the present community will have a much better chance of reaching people than an attempt to attract neighbors to the existing service(s).

My Paradigm of Priorities

I must say one thing that is foundational to my writing this book: I believe the most important priority of the local church is to continue Christ's mission to make disciples.

There are other things a church can and should be doing. But nothing is on a par with this singular mission of the church. Call it evangelism, church growth, outreach, disciple making. It doesn't matter. The bottom line is that people outside the Christian community need to be the central focus for which the church exists. Just as Christ came to seek and to save those who are lost (Luke 19:10), the church is equally responsible to seek and to save those who are lost.

Unfortunately, half of all churches in North America did not add even one new member last year through conversion. That fact alone should be enough to convince us that we must explore additional strategies for fulfilling Christ's mission. I strongly believe there is only one thing the church *must* do, and that is to carry on Christ's own mission.

After that, I'm easy. You can immerse or sprinkle, close or open communion, speak in tongues or stick to English. The apostle Paul's words reflect my own: "I have become all things to all [people] so that by all possible means I might save some" (1 Cor. 9:22). As Donald McGavran, founder of the modern church growth movement, would regularly tell his students, "It's God's will that his Church grow, that his lost children be found." The principles—and the benefits—of adding a new service work across theological lines, geographical boundaries, and denominational convictions. But the common denominator must be a motivation to reach lost men and women for Jesus Christ and disciple them into his church.

Let's Begin Our Journey

I hope you enjoy yourself while reading this book. Keep a yellow marker handy; make lots of notes. I have spent much of the last three years collecting research and conducting interviews for this book. As a result, I am convinced that a powerful strategy of church growth for thousands of churches across North America is to start a new service. I think you'll find lots of good, practical information in this book. And if you decide to become involved in this cutting-edge experience, I can promise you renewed excitement in ministry, increased involvement in membership, and a revitalized commitment to the mission of seeing new people come to a life-changing faith in Jesus Christ.

Why Start
a New Service?

Let me share with you seven reasons why your church should add a new style worship service in the next twelve to twenty-four months. Whether you have one service, two, three, or more, the reasons for—and value of—adding a new service do not change. You may respond to one reason in particular. Others in your church may find a different one more compelling. In reality, a shared congregational motive for beginning a new service is not important. What is important is a shared congregational goal—namely, to begin a new style service within the next two years.

When you introduce the idea of a new service to those in your church, the more reasons you present, the more likely members will hear at least one that convinces them to support the idea. Any one of these reasons is an adequate motive for a new service. In concert, I believe they form an absolute mandate.

Reason 1: A New Service Will Reach the Unchurched

Of all the reasons to begin a new service, this should be the most compelling. Over 152,500 churches in America did not add a single new convert last year, and 260,000 churches are currently plateaued or declining in worship attendance. For these churches in particular, reaching non-Christians should be cause enough to start a new service.

Christ's passion for reaching lost humanity is stated frequently and emphatically throughout Scripture:

"I must preach the good news of the kingdom of God to the other towns also, because that is why I was sent" (Luke 4:43).

"The Son of Man came to seek and to save what was lost" (Luke 19:10).

"God did not send his Son into the world to condemn the world, but to save the world through him" (John 3:17).

"The Son of Man did not come to be served, but to serve, and to give his life as a ransom for many" (Matt. 20:28).

"I have come that they may have life, and have it to the full" (John 10:10).

Not only was Jesus crystal clear about his own mission, he was definitive in his instructions to his followers concerning their task:

"'Come, follow me,' Jesus said, 'and I will make you fishers of men'" (Mark 1:17).

"The gospel must first be preached to all nations" (Mark 13:10).

"This gospel of the kingdom will be preached in the whole world as a testimony to all nations, and then the end will come" (Matt. 24:14).

"Go into all the world and preach the good news to all creation" (Mark 16:15).

"Repentance and forgiveness of sins will be preached in his name to all nations, beginning at Jerusalem" (Luke 24:47).

"You will receive power when the Holy Spirit comes on you; and you will be my witnesses in Jerusalem, and in all Judea and Samaria, and to the ends of the earth" (Acts 1:8).

Of all Christ's instructions to his followers, the one most often quoted, which was given as a summary of his entire purpose on earth, is what many call the Great Commission: "Go and make disciples of all nations, baptizing them in the name of the Father and of the Son and of the Holy Spirit, and teaching them to obey everything I have commanded you. And surely I am with you always, to the very end of the age" (Matt. 28:19–20).

The first reason for starting a new service—and by far the most important—is that a new service will increase the number of people you reach with the gospel of Jesus Christ.

Why is this so?

A. A new service will focus your church's attention on the unchurched. Starting a new service has many similarities to starting a new church. Those who have been part of planting a new church know the strong sense of mission, group spirit, and excitement that is found in planning to reach new people with the gospel. These dynamics also occur when a church becomes involved in starting a new service. Like a new church, a new service focuses on people not presently involved in a church. Members must ask, Who is the new service for? Why are we starting a new service? How are these new people going to be reached? These questions—and their answers—lead a congregation beyond its own walls to the unchurched.

B. A new service will help you repackage your message. Rev. Arnell ArnTessoni, director of new church development for the American Baptist Churches, says it this way: "In order to reach our communities with the unchanging truth and love of Jesus Christ, we may be required to remove the cultural wrapping in which we have cloaked the Good News. Frequently it is not the Word of God people are rejecting as irrelevant. It is the outdated clothing in which we have dressed our Lord."[1]

Certain forms and liturgies become almost sacred to those who have grown up with them. For many sincere and well-meaning folks, there is only one right way to worship, one right music to sing and play, one right time and right day to have church. Anything other than the familiar worship patterns will never seem right to them.

I was confronted with an example of this conflict between ritual and relevance several years ago while conducting a seminar

25

in North Carolina for Southern Baptist pastors. The topic was worship that attracts the unchurched. I suggested that a modern translation would help make the gospel more understandable to people who had not read a Bible recently—in other words, some version other than the King James. I was immediately informed by a number of those in attendance that if they were to try such an idea, the following Sunday they would be looking for a new job!

Perhaps in your church it is not the Bible translation that is sacred. Perhaps it is the rising and singing of the doxology following the offering. Perhaps it is the worship service that must begin at 11:00 A.M. Sunday morning. Maybe it is the requirement that the pastor wear a robe, or that communion be held on the first Sunday of each month, or that a salvation invitation be given at the conclusion of each service.

Starting a new service will force your church to ask an important question: What is our form, and what is our essence? What are the changeable conventions by which we conduct church activities, and what are the essential ingredients that compose our unchanging message? Many unchurched people who are put off simply by the form of religion are otherwise receptive to the essence of Christ and the gospel. Starting a new service allows you to shed cultural or sociological forms that may be keeping you from effectively reaching a new group of people.

C. A new service will allow your members to invite their friends. Research shows that the primary way churches grow is by members inviting their friends and relatives.[2] However, most members of nongrowing churches do not invite anyone.[3] Why? Because they don't believe their friends or relatives would find the service interesting or relevant. When a church offers a new service that is relevant, appropriate, and well presented, a dramatic increase is shown in the number of invitations church members extend to others.

So to summarize the first reason for starting a new service, churches that start one will reach more unchurched people. Unfortunately, not all people find this to be a compelling reason. So let's look at a second reason.

26

Reason 2: A New Service Will Minister to More People

Eighty percent of the congregations that move from one worship experience to two find their overall attendance jumps by at least 10 percent.[4] Whether the new service is on Saturday for the 27 percent of working Americans who cannot attend every Sunday or is on Thursday evening for Baby Boomers taking weekend minivacations, whether the new service is for those who prefer contemporary music or for parents who want to worship with their children in a family service, the more options you provide, the more people you will reach.

People today want choices—in their cars, their cereals, their detergents, their television programs. Businesses know that the more variety of products they offer, the more people will select one of them. Coca Cola offers nine choices of Coke. Ford offers seven lines of cars, with a wide variety of colors and interior options for each. This insight is crucial for churches in today's world of choices. Offering only one service, at one time of day, on one day of the week, with one style, says to your community, "This is your choice—take it or leave it." Guess which option most will choose?

But when the decision is no longer "take it or leave it," but "when," "what," "how," or "where," you greatly increase people's choices. And the more choices you provide for a worship service, the more people will say yes to one of them. This principle of multiple choices has been practiced for years in the Roman Catholic church. Drive by a Catholic parish some day and count the number of times and days one can attend mass. The pope knows something: People like choices!

The importance of providing worship service choices can be visually illustrated through the following diagrams. When your church has only one service per week, the choice of responses you are giving to people is simple: "yes to this service" or "no to this service" (fig. 2).

27

Figure 2

Alternative Responses Available

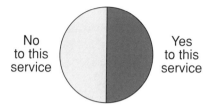

But when you offer two services, you have doubled the number of opportunities you now give people to say yes and increased the statistical likelihood of a positive response to one of your services from 50 percent to 66 percent (fig. 3).

Figure 3

Alternative Responses Available

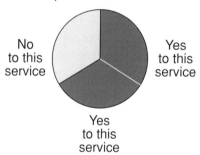

Offer three services and you triple the number of choices and increase the opportunities to say yes to 75 percent. This does not mean that 75 percent of those you invite to a service will come. It means that when you have three services, you have a 75 percent better chance of seeing those who are invited actually attend (fig. 4). And the percentage increases with additional services beyond even three.

People do not join a church without first visiting. One essential part of any church's growth equation, therefore, is simply hav-

28

Figure 4

Alternative Responses Available

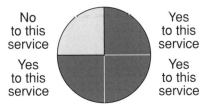

| No to this service | Yes to this service |
| Yes to this service | Yes to this service |

ing enough visitors. Because more people will say yes to visiting your church when you add a new service, more members is a normal consequence.

The national "visitor retention rate" is 8 to 12 percent. That is, most churches see 8 to 12 percent of their first-time visitors become active members in the following year. Given one hundred visitors per year at a 10 percent retention rate, a church will add ten new members in a year. But 10 percent of two hundred visitors means twenty new members. It's a simple matter of mathematics: More visitors means more members. And more services means more visitors.

Reason 3: A New Service Will Reach New Kinds of People

A new style service will not only help you reach more non-Christians (reason 1) and help you minister to more total numbers of people (reason 2), it will help you reach different kinds of people than you are presently reaching.

Here's why. The worship service is the primary "door of entrance" for people to become involved in congregational life. Visitors decide to become active in a church based primarily on their experience in and around the worship service. And like it or not, your service is attractive to some people while not attractive to others. "The simple truth is that worship cannot be culturally neutral," says James White.[5] No single service can be all things to

29

all people. Consequently, it is most important to ask, Who finds our present service(s) attractive?

Most church services in America are appealing to one (and generally only one) of six groups. While each group can be further defined (and will be later in this book), the grid in figure 5 can help you consider the people to whom your existing service is attractive. And by default it will identify those who do not find your service attractive.

Figure 5

To Whom Is Your Present Service Most Attractive?

	Generational Group		
	Baby Busters (born 1965–78)	Baby Boomers (born 1946–64)	Seniors (born before 1946)
Christian			
Seeker			

(Spiritual Condition)

One style of service will not effectively reach or minister to a large number of people in more than one of these six segments. If you desire to increase attendance in your existing service(s), the best strategy is to find and focus on people in your community who are in the same category as those already composing a majority of your present audience. But if you desire to reach new kinds of people in your community (from a different "people group" than is attending your present service), you will need a new service with a style focused on this new group.

For example, if you are presently attracting primarily Senior Christians in your existing service(s), you will need a new service to attract a significant number of Baby Boomer Christians. If you are already attracting Boomer Christians and your desire is to reach unchurched people (seekers) from that same age group, a new service will be much more successful than an attempt to attract them to your present service(s).

A mistake some churches make in an effort to broaden the generational and/or spiritual range of people attracted to their existing service(s) is to diversify the music or liturgical style. In so doing, however, most churches actually diminish the effectiveness of their present service(s) among every people group, including their predominant one.

Reason 4: A New Service Will Help Break the Normal Life Cycle

The life cycle of a church is both normal and predictable.[6] Like gravity, it is a law that simply exists. And like it or not, all churches—including yours—are subject to it. The life cycle describes a local church's infancy, maturity, and death. The sober-

Figure 6

Typical Church Life Cycle

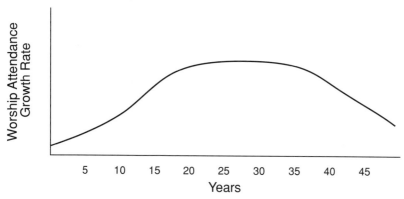

31

ing fact is that at least 80 percent of the churches in America today are on the flat or back side of their life cycles.[7]

Figure 6 represents a typical church life cycle. In the early stages of a church's life, there is a high sense of mission among all involved. The church is purpose driven. Charter members, and often even the pastor, volunteer their time to help the church reach people and grow. Buildings are less important; structure is less important. The motivation is outreach, and the result is growth.

As the formative years give way to time, the church reaches a comfortable size and generally stops growing. If growth does continue, the percentage of transfer growth increases and the percentage of conversion growth declines. An emerging pattern of institutionalization is reflected in the increasing number of committees and the decreasing degree of accomplishment.

The final stage of the life cycle, decline, often begins around a church's fortieth to fiftieth birthday. Few, if any, members have the passion of the founders. The community has usually changed[8] but the church has not. Decline in worship attendance during this stage of the life cycle may be gradual or abrupt. Few in the church, including the staff, believe that the church's best days are still ahead.

But what about those churches that rise above this predictable life cycle pattern and experience growth beyond the first twenty to thirty years? How do they do it?

Figure 7

Most Churches Do Not Grow Like This

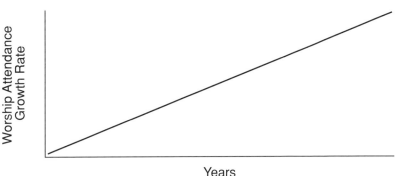

Figure 8

Most Churches Grow Like This

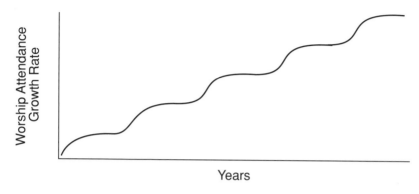

As I have studied and charted the growth of churches that don't fit the mold of a normal life cycle, a fascinating pattern has emerged. Rather than a constant or linear pattern of growth (fig. 7), growing churches that have broken out of their predictable life cycle reflect a stair-step pattern of growth (fig. 8).

Here's a key insight: Most churches that are growing when they would be plateaued or declining have begun new life cycles! Something has interrupted the church's normal pattern—I call it an "intervention event"—and a new life cycle has begun before the old life cycle has pulled the church into decline or death.

Below is a list of common intervention events that have been the cause of a new life cycle in many churches.[9] As you can see, most of these are controllable; some simply happen.

1. Change of pastors
2. Occurrence of a crisis
3. Planting of a church
4. Closing then reopening of the church
5. Renewal of pastor
6. Renewal of laity
7. Involvement of the denomination
8. Hiring of an outside consultant
9. Relocation of the church
10. Beginning a new service

33

Figure 9

Critical Points in a Church's Life Cycle

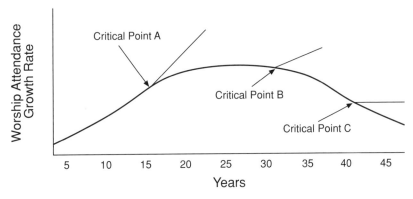

Of all the controllable intervention events that can help a church begin a new life cycle, the establishment of a new worship service is the most likely to do so. As I noted earlier, a new service brings a renewed sense of mission, enthusiasm, and anticipation—all qualities found in the beginning of a new lifecycle, but ones which easily fade as a church becomes more institutionalized. To state this more directly: *The best way to begin a new life cycle is to begin a new service.*

Depending on where your church is in its life cycle, there will be different numerical results from introducing a new service. Figure 9 identifies three critical points in a church life cycle and the effect of introducing a new service at each point.

Critical Point A

Introducing a new style service at this point in a church's life cycle is reasonably difficult. But it is ideally the best place to do so. The difficulty comes as lay leaders look at the present worship attendance—higher each year than the year before—and wonder whether the benefit of adding a different kind of service is worth the risk. Things seem to be going well with the existing service. If anything, it would seem that an additional identical service would be appropriate.

34

Despite the challenge of beginning a new service, a church that does so at critical point A will add at least ten years of growth to its present life cycle. For such churches, a new service retains the zest of youth that brought it this far. The new service serves as a booster rocket to maintain the momentum of growth and to continue the passion of mission. At this point a new service begins a new life cycle before the gravity of the old life cycle begins to pull the church out of its growth and mission mode. If a new church adds a new service even while its present service is still growing, the total growth pattern will continue farther into the future.

Critical Point B

If your church's growth has plateaued for the past ten to fifteen years (plus or minus 5 percent change in total worship attendance), adding a new service can be a positive intervention strategy to avoid the decline in attendance that will otherwise follow, and begin a new pattern of growth through a new life cycle.

It is at this point in a church's life cycle that it is actually easiest to gain congregational support for a new service. An assessment of the church's attendance pattern will generally confirm nongrowth. Because such churches have experienced growth in the relatively recent past and generally desire an increase in attendance, a new style service is likely to receive a positive response. The exception to this is if the church has its financial obligations met (perhaps through an endowment), the sanctuary is at least 50 percent full on an average Sunday, and the congregation has little need or desire to add new members.

Critical Point C

It's difficult to know exactly when a church reaches this point in its life cycle. In reality, it is the point of no return. If an intervention strategy is not introduced at this point, the church will slip beyond resuscitation.

For most churches at point C, it's better to conduct a major overhaul of the existing service than to add a new service. Adding a new service at a time when the resources and vision of the church are already stretched to the limit is not likely to succeed. Our Savior Lutheran Church (Santa Clara, Calif.) had been declining in attendance for the previous decade when they determined to add a new service in an effort to stop the decline. The result, however, was to exacerbate the problem rather than remedy it, and the church essentially divided its small congregation of about seventy-five in half. A year later they merged the two services but found that the difficulties of bringing two dissimilar services back together precluded a harmonious union.

Most churches at this point in the life cycle do not have the energy, vision, or resources to add an additional service. If the church is close to death, it is usually not difficult to obtain permission from the congregation for a major change in service style, since most members realize the choice is simple: Change or die.

Reason 5: A New Service Allows for Change While Retaining the Familiar

If you wish to reach out to and attract new groups of people to your church, you have essentially three options. Each option results in a fairly predictable outcome:

Option 1: Redesign your present service. This approach will indeed reach new people and potentially be the beginning of a new life cycle in a church. The cost, however, may be a considerable loss of members as people become unhappy and leave. (Not all of those who do, by the way, will leave peacefully or quietly.)

The loss of members, and the temporary destabilization of the church's equilibrium, may be a price you are willing to pay. And in fact, the people you lose may be ones you had hoped to lose years ago! A word to pastors, however, who pursue this option. Take a careful assessment of (1) your equity with church leadership, (2) your personal commitment to staying at the church for at least the next two years, and (3) your spouse's

36

commitment to you. While you may get lucky and find that the change from one style to another is easy, more likely you will be in for long and not particularly pleasant months of stress. If you prevail, the outlook is bright. You will have an almost entirely new church and hopefully be ready to begin a new life cycle.

Option 2: Incorporate more variety into your existing service. The usual goal of this strategy is to provide a service in which a broader range of people can experience something they like. A few old hymns mixed with contemporary praise songs with perhaps some 1960s choruses for the oldies crowd would seem to make everyone happy. But in an effort to provide a service in which everyone finds something they like, you will more likely discover you have created a service in which everyone finds something they don't like. And people tend to remember what they didn't like in a service much longer than what they did like. With this option, as with option 1, you will reach new people—namely, those who like a potpourri of experiences. But that number is a minority and probably fewer than the number you are reaching now, and it will be won at the price of losing some (perhaps many) attenders.

With options 1 and 2, incidentally, the financial implications should not go overlooked. Those members who will leave because of the change in style are frequently larger givers than the new people who will be attracted. One recent study in Florida found that seven new Baby Boomer members were required to financially replace every Senior adult member who left.[10]

Option 3: Add a service that offers a clear choice of styles. If you adopt this strategy, you will double your outreach and ministry potential, provide opportunities for more members to have a role or task in ministry, and see new kinds of people begin attending. Members will be far more likely to tolerate change around them if their own comfortable world is not disturbed.

This third option builds on an important principle of innovation that every church leader would do well to memorize: Change through addition will be more successful than change through substitution.

If church members feel they are losing something of value ("their" service), even though it may be for a seemingly worthwhile cause, many will resist it, believing that the benefit is not worth the cost. Through adding a new service without deleting your existing one, you double your outreach and ministry potential while allowing those members who prefer the present service to continue receiving their spiritual nourishment. My vote, in the vast majority of cases, is for option 3!

Reason 6: A New Service Will Activate Inactive Members

In studying churches that have added a new service, I have frequently observed a serendipitous benefit—the percentage of inactive members decreases. In the typical American church, approximately 40 percent of the membership attend a service on any given Sunday. Reasons for inactivity vary. But regardless of the cause, the people who stay away are nonverbally saying that the cost of attending (in time and/or comfort) is not worth the benefit (in spiritual growth and/or fellowship). It is not uncommon, however, to see a new service boost the member attendance percentages from the 40 percent range to 60 percent or more. In other words, some of the people most likely to begin attending your new service will be your inactive members.

Once a formerly active member stops attending church for longer than six months, it generally becomes too uncomfortable and too embarrassing for that person to return. A new service, however, provides a perfect excuse for many inactive members to give that church a second chance. While they won't usually return to the church they left, some inactive members will return to something new. When sensitively invited, 15 to 20 percent of resident inactive members can be expected to try your new service.

Earlier in this chapter I suggested that one reason for adding a new service is to reach a larger number of people. Some of those people will be returning inactive members.

38

Reason 7: A New Service Will Help Your Denomination Survive

Denominational church families that desire to be effective and vital in the twenty-first century must see a large percentage of their churches participating in one or both of two growth strategies: (1) the starting of new churches, and (2) the starting of new services.

There is little question among church growth scholars that starting new churches is the single most important activity for assuring the future of a denomination. But it is not as commonly known that the widespread creation of new services among existing churches is the second most important strategy. When a large number of churches in a denomination are starting a new service to reach a new target audience, they are in effect accomplishing many of the goals of, and realizing many of the benefits inherent in, planting a new church.

In Conclusion

Assuming you are convinced of the value of and need for adding a new service (perhaps you were before you began reading this chapter), the remainder of this book will examine how to do it right. Doing it right is indeed important. I have found that if a church endeavors to add a new service and (for whatever reason) fails, it will be at least three to four years before there will be enough of a consensus in the church to try it again.

So let's do it right. Here's how.

The Role
of the Pastor

If you are a pastor, it is important to realize that when you initiate and support a proposal for a new style service, you will be wagering a significant amount of "leadership equity" on the outcome. A successful new service will immeasurably strengthen your influence in every aspect of the church for years to come. A highly visible and obvious failure risks losing it all.

It is also important to realize, as a pastor, that a halfhearted commitment to a new service is more likely to cause the service to fail than to succeed.[1] You are the one critical individual who needs a clear and firm conviction that God wants your church to add a new service and to reach new people. You will need to provide the spark. You will need to fan the flame. And you will need to keep the fire burning during the first critical year.

Do You Have What It Takes?

The pastor's role is critical in successfully adding a new service. Before you make a public commitment, search your own heart to see if you have the following.

A Conviction That This Is God's Will

As the church's spiritual leader, you must become the prophet, articulating God's will to reach new people. Therefore a clear and certain conviction of God's will is absolutely essential. No small amount of prayer and study should precede your formal presentation of the idea of a new service to church leadership. Seek God's heart and be certain it is his will, not just your desire.

Different people talk with and listen to God in different ways. I would suggest that as part of this process, you convene a special leadership prayer group to help you seek God's will. Personally invite six to eight people whom you respect for their faith and insight to join you once a week for at least one month of prayer and study on this topic.

If your church has helped members study and discover their spiritual gifts, an ideal representation of spiritual gifts in this leadership prayer group would be:

- *Intercession*—the special ability God gives to certain members of the body of Christ to pray for extended periods of time on a regular basis and see frequent and specific answers to their prayers, to a degree much greater than that which is expected of the average Christian.
- *Faith*—the special ability God gives to certain members of the body of Christ to discern with extraordinary confidence the will and purposes of God for his work.
- *Missionary*—the special ability God gives to certain members of the body of Christ to minister whatever other spiritual gifts they have in a second culture.
- *Knowledge*—the special ability God gives to certain members of the body of Christ to discover, accumulate, analyze, and clarify information and ideas which are pertinent to the well-being of the body.[2]

Even if you have not identified the spiritual gifts of members, you may be able to intuitively select men and women on the basis of these qualities.

In addition, it is wise to include the president of the congregation (chairperson of the board, clerk of session, etc.) as a member of the group. Invite several new members who have leadership potential. And if there are members that you will need as allies if the church moves ahead in this step of faith, invite them to be a part of the prayer group, as well. (Appendix A provides suggestions, activities, and recommended Bible study passages for these prayer group meetings.)

The goal of this prayer group is for you, as pastor, to receive corroboration from these saintly people that God is indeed leading in this direction. (Of course, if you do not, it should give you serious pause.) If you feel there is a consensus that God would have the church move ahead in this area, ask group members to continue praying individually for you and other church leaders as you take the next step in pursuing God's will.

A Vision of a Better Tomorrow

To pastor a growing church, you need not be a charismatic superstar. But there is increasing evidence that to pastor a growing church, you must have a clear vision of where you believe God is calling the church to go.[3] "Not much happens without a dream," says Robert Greenleaf in *The Win Arn Growth Report*. "And for something great to happen there must always be a great dream. Behind every great achievement is a dreamer of great dreams. Much more than a dream is required to bring it to reality; but the dream must be there first."[4]

Adding a new style service demands a pastor with a vision of the church accomplishing greater things for God than it presently is accomplishing. This dream must be as restless as a caged lion, pacing, prowling, constantly looking for a means of escape. And that same passion must be exhibited to the leaders and congregation, for it will be the vision of a better tomorrow that will motivate the church to risk a departure from the comfort of today. "I propose that the missing ingredient in developing multiple worship services," observes Carl George, "is not the lack of new people but the lack of a compelling drive to reach an enlarged harvest."[5]

What are the risks for which a strong vision will be required? Rev. Hylyard Irvin, pastor of the Glendale First Church of the Nazarene (Glendale, Ariz.) shares the difficulties he experienced when the church decided to add a new service: "There are major problems that can occur. You are creating two services which, in essence, becomes two churches. There will be a different spirit that will prevail that will be totally different. Another problem will be the criticism of your traditionalists. It will stretch your music budget. It will stress your ministerial staff. Your board needs to give consideration to taking things off the staff and allowing lay people to assume some of the responsibilities. I strongly suggest that you help your pastor with a prayer support team to pray for him before each preaching service, since it will be exhausting for him."[6]

The work to begin the new service will require considerable energy on the part of the pastor. It is the vision of what God will do through changed lives in the new service that is the only adequate source for that energy. Donald McGavran, founder of the modern church growth movement, once observed of growing churches that "it is a vision that compels the pilgrimage."[7] The pastor's single most important responsibility is to understand the vision God has for that church and then communicate it to God's people. It's a timeless principle: Without a vision the people perish. It is a critical ingredient in successfully starting a new service.

The Necessary Personality Type

Many tests have been developed to identify and categorize personality types. The Myers-Briggs Type Indicator (MBTI) and the Performax Personal Profile System (PPS) are two of the more popular. There appear to be certain pastoral personality types that are more inclined to initiate change in a church. And introducing a new style service certainly qualifies as change. If your personality and character traits are qualities common to change agents, it is likely that you will find the process of adding a new service exciting and challenging. If your personality type is not one of those types correlated with successful innovation, it does not mean you should abandon God's vision. But knowing your personality type

44

will help you to understand your spiritual, emotional, and psychological attitudes throughout the process.

So what are the personality traits that can be allies in adding a new service? While no specific studies have correlated personality types with success in adding a new service, there are studies and authoritative observations that are relevant.

A nationwide study by the Christian Churches/Churches of Christ used the Performax PPS to correlate personality types of church planters with subsequent growth of the new churches. The four primary personality types in the PPS are *dominance* ("motivated by results and challenge, strengths in initiating, getting results, accepting risks, decisiveness"), *influence* ("strong verbal skills, good with people, enthusiastic, able to influence others"), *steadiness* ("strong relational skills, ability to specialize, good listener, stable and supportive"), *compliance* ("commitment to excellence, methodical, focuses on details, critical objective thinker, able to follow directions").

The study correlated two personality types with the success of new churches. Because beginning a new church has many similarities with beginning a new service, the results are particularly interesting. Pastors who scored high on the dominance and/or influence portions of the test reported over twice the average worship attendance size as those pastors who scored high on the steadiness and compliance portions. The study went on to suggest that the dominance- and influence-oriented pastors had a higher level of personal satisfaction with their ministry, lower marital stress, and a greater sense of spiritual growth because of their work.

A related study found that these same two personality types—dominance and influence—were also more common in pastors who were successful in church revitalization efforts. A research study evaluated Baptist General Conference pastors who had successfully turned their churches from decline to growth, and found that these revitalization pastors had "a positive 'D' [dominance temperament] and a very high positive 'I' [influence temperament], along with a negative 'S' [steadiness temperament] and a negative 'C' [compliance temperament]."[8]

Beginning a new service is often a key part of revitalizing a declining church. I believe both studies suggest that the PPS per-

45

sonality types of dominance and influence will contribute to a pastor's successfully leading a church in starting a new service. Of course, there are exceptions to this generalization. The above study found that there was "an 84 percent certainty" that people with dominance and influence personality types would succeed in church revitalization. Just as it is possible to fail with the "right" personality type, it is possible to succeed against the odds. But realize that in some cases the odds may not be on your side.

Aubrey Malphurs uses the Myers-Briggs Type Indicator to identify pastoral personality types most likely to press for and lead change in their church. He notes that "the NT [intuitive-thinking] combination is the temperament best designed for change. NT pastors are strong, visionary leaders who are agents of change."[9] Intuitive people tend to take in information holistically, preferring the world of ideas, possibilities, and relationships. They are visionaries who thrive on change and new ideas. Thinking people tend to make their decisions on the basis of logic and objective analysis. They prefer to win people over by their logic, and take a more impersonal approach to decision making.

In combination these characteristics—intuitive and thinking—are strong allies to a pastor with a vision to begin a new service in his or her church. In contrast, pastors with the SJ (sensing and judging) character traits, as measured by the MBTI, tend to resist change and may find it a greater challenge to take the step of beginning a new style service.

An Ego

I cannot implant into your heart the correct motive for beginning a new service. Hopefully it is a godly vision to positively change lives. I hope your primary incentive is a commitment to honor Christ in building his church. This is ultimately the motive I believe God will bless through the life and health and growth of your new service.

This said, there are also additional ingredients that in my experience seem to motivate a fair number of pastors of growing churches. Hopefully they are secondary motives, but they are significant nonetheless. One of the most fascinating is ego.

It has been my opportunity, for which I thank God regularly, to meet and observe pastors representing a wide variety of theological persuasions, church sizes, and growth rates. A disproportionate number of pastors of large and/or complex churches, I have observed, seem to have larger-than-average egos. Pastors of churches at the cutting edge of creative ministry have big dreams for their church. They have to maintain the church's size and momentum. But they also seem to frequently have big dreams for themselves. I used to wonder why God would bless these people, who seem to thrive in the limelight of fame and success. Why didn't more quiet, kindhearted, meek, unassuming men and women of God rise to the top of the megachurch heap?

I am increasingly inclined to believe, however, that a large ego may actually be an asset in building a large church. I do know that most pastors of large and/or growing churches are not primarily motivated by ego gratification. These men are leading growing churches because of their conviction that God's Good News should be preached to everyone. Their primary motive is to positively touch the lives of large numbers of people through the church. The bigger the church, the more lives are being touched. But larger-than-normal egos seem to contribute to the realization of those dreams.

So what is the point? The point is that if you are a pastor and if your priorities are in order—God's priorities are first and foremost—then a degree of personal satisfaction in building a larger institution and a wider reputation in your community or denomination is not entirely harmful.

It may be something like the combination of gases in our atmosphere that we need to breathe. Most of our air is oxygen—78 percent. But there is also a certain amount of nitrogen mixed in—18 percent—which is necessary for our lungs to function and keep us alive. (The remainder, if you're adding, are miscellaneous gases.) Breathing pure nitrogen will kill a person in a few moments. But pure oxygen without some nitrogen is also insufficient to sustain human life over the long term. Perhaps this would approximate a healthy ratio of a pastor's motives for adding a new service: 78

47

percent God-centered and others-centered, 18 percent self-centered. (The remainder may be miscellaneous gases.)

I realize I run the risk of being misinterpreted on this point. I hope and pray that does not happen. The major and primary motive for beginning a new service must be one of reaching more people with the gospel. That is number one. It must always remain so. But I do not believe it is inappropriate for a pastor to also have a secondary motive related to his or her professional career as a leader in the Christian community. In fact, pastors who have a desire to lead a great church are more motivated to pay the higher price of time, energy, and effort required to build that church into an increasingly complex organization.

The Role of Initiator

One of the paradigms of pastoral leadership taught in many seminaries is: The pastor is an enabler. In this model the pastor enables laity for the work of ministry. No doubt, such an equipping role is biblical and appropriate. However, Win Arn observes:

> The view that "leaders are enablers" has inadvertently led to a stunting of growth in many unsuspecting churches. The reason is that "enabling," "equipping," and/or "facilitating" often results in a reactive style of leadership on the part of the pastor and staff. In such a mode, leaders look to the congregation for direction and then seek to support (enable) laity in their own agenda.
>
> In contrast, pastors of churches that are aggressively pushing the ministry envelope into new areas [and those that will be most successful in beginning a new service] seem to have adopted a leadership style that is less "enabler" and more "initiator." Their leadership style is *pro-active* rather than re-active. They *generate* ideas rather than respond to problems. In such approaches to church leadership, committees approve recommendations more often than initiate them. Members support ideas more often than suggest them. The pastor and staff are responsible to provide the spark.[10]

The church that has become accustomed to a pastor functioning as an enabler will be less likely to follow his or her lead in a

48

new worship service initiative than the church in which the pastor has operated as an initiator.

What Is the Cost?

There are numerous benefits to beginning a new service. Many were mentioned in the previous chapter. But those benefits do not come without a price. Before committing to the pursuit of a new service, it is worthwhile to count the costs.

Fear

The Church of the Nazarene conducted a study of their churches that had added a new style service.[11] The greatest obstacle pastors faced in deciding whether to move forward was fear. Fear of what? Here are the things identified as most commonly feared by pastors contemplating a new service:

- Lack of cooperation from people
- A small crowd
- Losing the dynamics of one large service
- Physical demands
- Psychological letdown of going from a crowded sanctuary to one that is half full
- Separate congregations
- Low morale
- Conflict with people resisting change

The same survey found that fear was not limited to the clergy and staff. Church boards also experienced fear when contemplating a new service. Uppermost on the list of things feared:

- Physical toll on the pastor
- Loss of unity
- Two separate congregations; not knowing everyone

49

- Effect of lower attendance in the worship service
- The new and different
- Drop in attendance

Yet among those churches that are now offering a new service, the study found that 100 percent of the respondents indicated that their congregations now felt positive toward the new service and that it was worth the time, money, and risk involved.

The Risk of Failure

Here is a principle of pastoral survival they didn't teach in seminary: You will not risk your career by tending to business as usual. Activities such as calling on hospitalized members, preparing and preaching respectable sermons, avoiding or resolving conflicts, and attending church meetings keep most pastors in their present position for as long as they feel called to stay.

But leading a church into change is risky business. And for most churches, adding a new service means both considerable change and considerable risk. As a pastor, you place yourself in the position of supporting what may be a highly visible failure. If the new service is a bust and is unceremoniously terminated, you can become a lame duck facing increased difficulty in generating support for future ideas. "The primary barrier to starting another service," says Elmer Towns, "is fear of failure. Because starting a second service may disrupt the most valued aspect of a church there may be more fear of it than any other change."[12]

The Risk of Success

Of course, a new service that does become a grand success is not risk free either. If you have designed and promoted a service that is meeting needs and attracting people, it is quite likely that attendance at the new service will not only grow but surpass the attendance of your established service. In churches that have had only one service or style for ten years or more, the success of a new service may cause greater consternation among the present membership than its failure. If the service is successful, the pastor risks the reaction of those who have sanctified the status quo.

While the real issues may or may not actually be verbalized (or even consciously understood), some of the following concerns regarding a successful new service will be in the minds of long-term members:

- Will "those people" ever start attending *real* church?
- Are we compromising the gospel and/or our theology just to get a crowd?
- I may lose the power and prestige I have established in this church.
- "Their" agenda will take the place of "our" agenda.
- Our facilities can't accommodate all the new people, and we will face the hassle of a building program.
- My financial contributions will be used for activities and expenses for which I receive no benefit.
- Will we lose the church in which we have so many memories?
- More people mean more problems and more work; with what real benefits?
- Will the pastor's attention and passion be focused on the new service at the price of lower quality in our service?
- We used to be one family; we are losing our closeness and sense of community.
- Those new people demand too much and give too little.

Obviously, the battle is not won a few months after your new service has established a critical mass and seems to be building momentum. The risk of a successful service, in fact, does not fully subside until eight to twelve months after attendance in the new service surpasses attendance in the established service.

Figure 10 depicts the pastor's exposure to risk, and even job security, when adding a new service. This risk begins with the initial public introduction of the idea of a new service. The level of risk varies throughout the process until one year after attendance at the new service surpasses attendance at the original service.

Figure 10

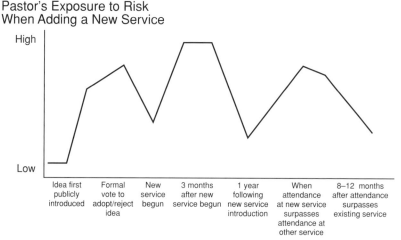

Pastor's Exposure to Risk
When Adding a New Service

| Idea first publicly introduced | Formal vote to adopt/reject idea | New service begun | 3 months after new service begun | 1 year following new service introduction | When attendance at new service surpasses attendance at other service | 8–12 months after attendance surpasses existing service |

Take a personal inventory of your willingness to put your reputation and leadership on the line in the pursuit of a new service. Introducing and championing a new service is one of the best ways to increase your leadership equity. But it is no small risk and no small decision.

Resistance to Change

Adding a new style service and focusing on a new target audience disrupts the equilibrium and status quo of a church. By definition, it is change. And human nature resists change, particularly in the church.

Why is it that people don't like to change? The following is adapted from the work of Aubrey Malphurs and applied specifically to the issue of adding a new service. It is helpful in understanding why people may resist your change initiatives.[13]

1. *Some people don't feel a need to change.* A new service, many church members feel, is unnecessary. There are still considerable numbers of empty pews, and the content of the present service is quite acceptable.

52

2. *Many people prefer the status quo.* One of the best things about your present service is that it's predictable. Every week it is the same day, the same time, the same routine. And predictability is one of the most alluring qualities of the status quo. For many members, predictability is not only desirable, it is the foundation of the church.

3. *A few cling to vested interests.* A new service will mean a loss of power for some members who have built up control and authority in the church.

4. *Some distrust leadership.* Particularly if the pastor is of a different generation than lay leadership in the church, there may be a sense that the pastor is not representing the best interests of the other generation.

5. *Change is stressful.* People know instinctively that change causes instability. A new and different service, particularly one that smacks of "worldly" things, is a threat to some in the church.

6. *Some things have become sacred in their own right.* For those who have grown up in the church and known only one liturgy of worship and one style of music, anything different is disrespectful to almighty God. As the crusades of the twelfth century clearly show, misdirected opinions can be inflamed by the conviction that "our way is God's way."

Yet without change the church becomes outdated, and in only a few short generations, irrelevant. Already 66 percent of Americans believe the traditional church is irrelevant.[14] Leith Anderson observes that the church in America is dying for lack of change.[15] If the members of your congregation believe that your church's purpose includes reaching unchurched people and bringing them into the community of faith, then you, as pastor, must convince your congregation that the question is not whether to change but simply what to change.

As you consider the likelihood of your people following your change initiative, it is helpful to realize there is a relationship between the length of time you have been in your position and the

Figure 11

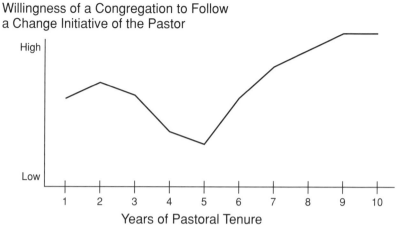

Willingness of a Congregation to Follow
a Change Initiative of the Pastor

willingness of your congregation to follow your leadership into the battle called change. Figure 11 illustrates this relationship.

If you have been in your church for less than two years, there is a reasonably good chance that the church will support your change initiative. The "honeymoon" is still fresh in the minds of members. They have little desire to rub their new pastor the wrong way on his or her first major initiative in the church (particularly if the agony of the pastoral calling process is still fresh in their minds).

But the confidence of members in the staying power of their pastor begins to wane around the third year. The average tenure of American pastors is 3.7 years. The unspoken fear of some in the church is that if they embark on a risky venture into the unknown, the pastor may find that things are too tough to keep going, and leave. The church is then burdened with the vision of a person who is no longer there.

If you are a pastor and have been in your church between three and five years (the lowest points in fig. 11), it does not mean you should not initiate a new service. It simply means that it is particularly important for you to solicit strong support among established lay leaders for the idea of a new service and assure them of your commitment to stay through and beyond the time required to get the service up and running. At this point in your tenure, you need allies to go into the battle with you; allies who are respected lay leaders.

If you have been in your church for over six years, your members' fear of losing their pastor begins to diminish. Particularly if you plan to stay for a long time—and tell them so—members' confidence that you will stick with a risky initiative causes them to be inclined to follow you into this new venture of faith. As a rule, the longer a pastor has been in the church after the fifth or sixth year, the more likely the members are to endorse his or her leadership initiatives.

It is not within the scope of this book to discuss all the dynamics of successful innovation and change in a church. Several excellent texts are available that deal entirely with this topic, and I recommend them to you.[16] Suffice it to say here that if and when you introduce the idea of a new service to your church, you are wise to be familiar with the dynamics of introducing and managing change.

More Time, More Work

A few years ago I was in Memphis with a group of Presbyterian pastors who had agreed to be part of a pilot project involving the creation of a new service. We were in the first of three meetings for this year-long project. After I had presented what I felt was a reasonable case for the value and benefits of a new service, a pastor in the back row asked, "What about all the extra time and work this will take?" I responded that indeed it would take additional effort by the pastor but that hopefully he felt the benefit of growth and extended ministry was worth it. I could tell by his body language that he wasn't convinced. A year later he still wasn't. The church had not even attempted to begin a new service because (in my estimation) the pastor had decided it wasn't worth the effort.

The fact is that a new service is going to take more work and more time than you are currently devoting to the worship portion of your ministry. The time required to plan and prepare for an effective new service is approximately four times what most pastors take to plan and prepare for their present service(s). This does not mean that the pastor should bear the sole burden for planning the service. Later we will look at the worship team as a recommended approach to planning an effective new service. But the pastor is a part of that worship team, and it will indeed take time. Ed Dobson, pastor of Calvary Church (Grand Rapids, Mich.), found that the contemporary seeker service took more time to plan than the other four traditional services combined.[17]

The additional time a pastor must devote to a new service, however, is not as great as one might suspect. In fact, most of the additional time required will be spent before the first new service is ever conducted. There will be the process of defining and researching the target audience for the new service, searching for and coordinating qualified musicians, identifying appropriate themes, promoting the service, and other important groundwork that occurs prior to the first service being held.

The additional time required by the pastor, once the new service is up and running, is primarily in attending worship planning meetings for the new service, not in sermon preparation. One recent survey found that when churches offered two or more different service styles, 94 percent of the time the sermons were identical.[18] Keep in mind, however, that a common denominator of successful services is highly relevant sermons. If your sermons resonate with that quality, the new service (as well as the old) is likely to grow.

Different pastors have developed different time schedules for selecting and preparing sermon topics. As a rule, the more people involved in the worship program, the more lead time is necessary in selecting the topic. Music, drama, and media teams may require six to ten weeks lead time or more. The Wooddale Church (Minneapolis, Minn.) where Leith Anderson is pastor, identifies and publishes themes a year in advance to allow the drama and music teams time to develop appropriate material.

The good news is that any additional time required for planning the new service may well be a blessing. Here's why: Pastors of growing churches generally don't put in a great deal more work time than pastors of nongrowing churches. The difference is that pastors of growing churches have learned to work smart, not just hard. They invest their time in areas that produce growth.[19] Time spent planning an excellent new service is a good example of working smart. Consequently, if you need to delegate some tasks that you suspect are less productive and/or could be done equally well by others, the new service can give you a perfect reason to do so.

Less Control

For some pastors the one hour of worship is a prized possession. He or she determines the sermon, selects the songs, approves the announcements, voices the prayer. It is a center stage experience. But with a new service, particularly one with a more contemporary style, control must be shared in two key areas:

1. *Service planning.* The selection of the service theme is best accomplished through a team of people familiar with the makeup of your target group. In addition, the selection of music, drama, media, and testimonies for the service is best delegated to the respective specialists on the worship planning team. The pastor should have final review of and veto power in regard to any ingredient in the service. But determining the scope and sequence of the service should not be the pastor's responsibility.

2. *Platform visibility.* In chapter 7 we will discuss the trend of churches utilizing a worship leader. This person emcees the service, calls the congregation to worship, provides bridges between segments, reads Scripture. The pastor is primarily responsible for bringing the sermon. This approach to worship has the benefit of involving more people, reducing dependency on one person, and maintaining people's attention in the pews. The consequence of this approach, however, is that the pastor is less the center of attention. For some pastors, that is not a desirable situation.

"It was a hard thing for me to do, turning over the planning of our new service to the worship team," says Rev. Chuck Laird of Westminster Presbyterian Church (Duluth, Minn.), which successfully added a new service. "And frankly, they made some mistakes. But their learning curve has increased tremendously, and now they are designing a service that has more creativity and effectiveness than I could have come up with on my own."[20]

More Stretch

If you have grown up with and known only one style and structure of worship, there is a good chance you will initially be uncomfortable participating in whatever new style of service is defined. Whether the new service is for a different generation, a different culture, or a different spiritual pilgrim than your present service is designed for, it will be a style with which you are probably unfamiliar. Your greatest discomfort will likely be with the music. But the issues and themes of the service, the dress, the day of the week, or the location will also likely be new and make you uncomfortable.

Commitment for Two Years

It will take approximately two years for a new service to become established as an accepted and normal part of your church's ministry. Prior to this point members will still perceive the new service to be in a test period, and that it may be discontinued if there are greater problems than benefits. Consequently, the new service requires regular and visible support by its champions (specifically the pastor) for the first two years.

If you, as pastor, leave before this incubation period for the new service has elapsed, the chances are high that the service will be discontinued. Figure 12 illustrates the probability of the new service being discontinued, based on when you leave the church.

A pastor of a Reformed Church in Los Angeles rightly concluded that his church needed a new contemporary service. He gathered together a group of both younger and older adults in a meeting of what later became the worship planning group. There was considerable excitement about the possibilities for new growth and outreach through the new service.

I received a phone call from the pastor three months into the project. He asked whether I thought the new service would be

Figure 12

Probability of the New Service Being
Discontinued If the Pastor Leaves the Church

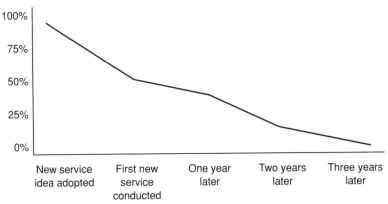

jeopardized if he were to accept a call to become the pastor of a church in Atlanta. I told him, "Probably so."

"But the committee has established real momentum, and the interim pastor is a creative person who would support the project," he responded.

I said I couldn't be sure, but his departure would certainly not help the prospects for the new service. As of this writing (one year after his departure), the chairman of the committee is struggling to keep the people involved, and while the interim pastor is supportive, he is hesitant to lead the church into something that may be uncertain and risky during his tenure. I hope this church succeeds; they need to in order to ensure their viability. But at the moment I would not bet on their success.

A Final Word

One could wonder, after reading this chapter, about the wisdom of moving ahead with a new service. Let me assure you, there is great wisdom in moving ahead. But there is also great wisdom in counting the cost and checking your account to be sure you can pay for it. If you decide to proceed—and I hope you do—you will find the benefit to be well worth the investment.

If and when you conclude that God is calling your church to move forward in establishing a new service, here is one final word of advice: Don't look back. You will have moments of doubt. You will wonder whether the cost was underestimated. But keep the vision in front of you. Keep looking to God as the source of your vision, and the resource to see the vision accomplished. Remember, it's not your idea, and it's not your church. It's God's. The words of Mordecai to Esther are God's words to you as well: "If you remain silent at this time, relief and deliverance . . . will arise from another place. . . . And who knows but that you have come to [the kingdom] for such a time as this" (Esther 4:14).

The benefit *is* worth the cost. The people who will be attracted to and touched by your new service will bring an invigorating new perspective to your personal life and ministry in a way nothing else can or will. You are called to your church—and the kingdom—for such a time as this. And in due time the Master will reward you with the words, "Well done, good and faithful servant."

Getting the Church on Board

A successful new service will have a tremendous positive effect on your church's corporate self-esteem. If and when the new service becomes a mainstay in your ministry, a "we can do it" attitude will surface in other areas of the church as well. Members will be more supportive of other faith-stretching initiatives based on the success of this endeavor.

The converse, unfortunately, is also true. If a new service is attempted and fails, the church's confidence in its ability to tackle other challenges also drops. It will be harder to get leaders to take steps of faith in other areas of the church's ministry and believe that God will bless their faithfulness.

Consequently, each step in the process of adding a new service should be thoughtfully examined and addressed. The first important step is getting church leaders on board.

Planning Your Strategy

Once you have personally concluded that it is God's will for your church to reach out into the community through a new style service, it is time to begin the process of moving the idea through the system of the church hierarchy, generating conviction and a sense of ownership of this exciting new step of faith.

People, by nature, tend to resist change. Consequently, how you introduce the idea of a new service will greatly affect whether it is eventually adopted. Do not assume that the idea will be naturally accepted on its obvious merits. It will not. In fact, you are much safer (and more likely to be correct) in assuming that the idea will be resisted. People are allergic to change.

In a national study on churches' responsiveness to change, Paul Mundey asked pastors what was the most difficult change they had attempted to make in their church. "Overwhelmingly," he reports, "respondents listed something connected with the worship or the Sunday morning schedule as the most difficult, including:

- the addition of a worship service, especially a contemporary one;
- a change in time for the existing worship service;
- a change in time for Sunday School;
- an attempt to introduce more contemporary elements into an existing worship service."[1]

One of the necessary steps in successfully moving a church toward the addition of a new service is, as Carl George puts it, "effective leadership that can do the political maneuvering necessary to rally the church in support of such new outreach."[2] Here are six guidelines for change that will serve you well in your presentation of the idea of a new service. They are, in fact, helpful principles anytime change should be made in the church and others must be convinced.

1. Introduce the idea as a way to reach an agreed-upon goal. One of the best reasons for a church to spend time developing and adopting a mission statement is so it will be ready when it is time for change. If there has been previous thought, discussion, and prayer put into a mission statement, and if the congregation has adopted this statement of purpose, subsequent ideas for change are more likely to be supported if they are positioned as a step toward that previously agreed-upon goal. In a church bulletin several years ago the First Nazarene Church (Pasadena, Calif.) included a "Question-Answer" insert prior to launching a contemporary worship service. The first question read:

> Question: Why are two worship service options being studied?
> Answer: Our mission statement states that we intend for ministry to be offered with a "diversity of options." This means any options that are offered take into consideration the needs of our church family and those of our community. Both experience and research indicate that a seeker-sensitive worship would allow us to have a significant impact on local people not now a part of our church fellowship, nor of any other church fellowship.[3]

2. Introduce the idea as an addition, not a replacement. Most people resist change not for fear of discovering the future but for fear of discarding the past. When you present the idea of a new service, members should be assured that the present service will not be changed. The goal is to offer more options so that more people have the opportunity to be a part of the body of Christ. Bear Valley Baptist Church (Denver, Colo.) has a successful Saturday night service. The pastor has said, "It would have been very difficult for us to change any of the traditional services on Sunday morning. Instead, we simply rented a jr. high auditorium and started another service."[4] You will have much more freedom to initiate a new service and try new approaches if those who attend the present service—and enjoy it—are not asked to give up their service as a result.

3. Introduce the idea as a short-term experiment, not a long-term commitment. Members who question whether the new service is an appropriate or wise move for the church will be more open to accepting a trial period, in which the new service is conducted and then evaluated. Agree on a date when the new service will be reviewed. At that time collectively evaluate whether the service is accomplishing its goals. If the service is in fact a successful step in the pursuit of the church's mission, it will be far easier at that time to obtain permission for a long-term commitment. If it is not

63

accomplishing its goals, it is to everyone's advantage to reconsider. (Chapter 9 will focus on evaluating the new service.)

Another benefit of an initial short-term view toward the new service is that we, as humans, are more tolerant of change if it is seen as a temporary condition. Then we often discover that the change is not as distasteful as we had feared and in fact is often more desirable than the past. Once members begin to accommodate the idea of their church offering an additional service, they will generally be more tolerant of continuing the service at the end of the experimental period.

"Respondent after respondent," reports Mundey, "shared that the strategy of a 'trial period' had made it much easier to introduce change. People knew that the change was not permanent and that there would be opportunity to evaluate what had been done. That greatly increases the openness of a congregation to experimentation. This strategy also helps those seeking the change because they don't have their necks stuck out so far! If the experiment doesn't work, no one has lost great dignity or reputation because of it."[5]

4. Encourage enhancements to create ownership. Good goals are my goals; bad goals are your goals. If a member feels that the goal of a new service is something in which he or she has a personal identity, that member will be more likely to support the idea and work for its success. Goal ownership comes through helping to formulate or refine the goal. Ask others for ideas on how the new service can be most effective. Encourage creativity in advertising and promotion. Solicit suggestions for themes and topics of the new service. In all likelihood the ideas will enhance the new service as well as broaden goal ownership.

5. Sow seeds of creative discontent. Here is a principle of change that applies to all of life, including the church: Voluntary change only occurs when there is sufficient discontent with the status quo. For many, the primary comfort of the church is its predictability. Things seem to be the same today as they have been for years. And it is that very stability that causes people to resist change in the church. "The solution," says Malphurs, "is to help those people and their churches discover that everything is not all right."[6] In generating support for the new service, seek to whet members' appetites to the greater ministry God desires and the larger number of people he wants to touch through the church. Point out that to simply continue along the present course will not, in all likelihood, result in the realization of such a dream.

There is a difference between destructive discontent and constructive discontent. Destructive discontent is a desire to leave the present for a more appealing past. Constructive discontent is a desire to leave the present for a more appealing future.

6. Start with the leaders. Convince your lay leaders to support the new service initiative, and it will become a reality. Elected leaders, particularly the church board, are your most strategic focus. The persuasion process must begin here. Ed Dobson recalls his first formal step in exploring a new service: "I decided to discuss my concerns with the board. I asked permission to get a small committee together to explore how we could reach more unchurched people. I talked about the old Youth for Christ rallies in the Grand Rapids area. Many of the board members had attended the rallies and had seen God work in miraculous ways. I suggested the idea of a YFC rally for the nineties. I was given permission to explore the idea and report back to the board."[7]

The men and women in positions of lay leadership are so central to the success of a new service that a significant portion of this chapter is devoted to the process of convincing them to support the initiative. With their support you have an alliance that will lead to churchwide adoption. Without their support you would be wise to move on to other issues.

How People Will Respond

I have noted that the pastor's role is critical to the success of a new service, and part of the role is that of initiator. Boards and committees can and should give endorsement to the initiative. But they will never be its champion. It should become the church's project, but it must be the pastor's initiative.

Therefore, it is helpful to understand and anticipate how people will respond to your idea of a new service. The response of individual members will fall into one of five categories and can be illustrated by the bell curve in figure 13.

Figure 13

How Members Will Respond to the Idea of a New Service

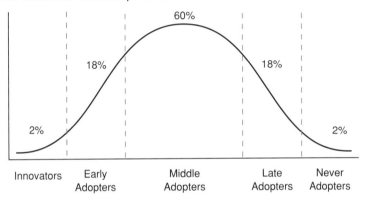

Innovators — Early Adopters — Middle Adopters — Late Adopters — Never Adopters

Innovators are the dreamers and visionaries in your church. They regularly talk about the future rather than the past but are not generally acknowledged as leaders or policy makers. Many have the spiritual gift of faith (1 Cor. 12:9).

Early Adopters are those who know a good idea when they see it. Their opinions are generally respected by others, and they are influential in moving the church forward in new directions. They often receive credit for ideas that were really not theirs. Many have the spiritual gift of wisdom (1 Cor. 12:8).

Middle Adopters make up the majority of the congregation. They tend to react to the ideas of others rather than generate their own. While these people are generally reasonable in their analysis of a new idea, they are inclined toward maintaining the status quo and are more easily influenced by those opposing change than by those supporting it.

Late Adopters are the last in a church to endorse a new idea. In congregational and committee meetings, these people often speak against and vote against proposed changes and new ideas. They may never verbally acknowledge acceptance of a new idea but will eventually go along if the majority agrees to support it.

Never Adopters are those who seldom if ever accept new ideas. Their commitment is to the status quo or the past. They often sow discord after change is adopted, and will eventually leave if they don't get a following.

Implications of the Bell Curve

Based on figure 13, here are several things to remember when you introduce the idea of a new service:

1. Realize that not everyone will be happy. Innovators are on a collision course with Never Adopters. Early Adopters are frustrated by the lack of vision of Late Adopters. And Middle Adopters may encourage this disagreement so they can adequately consider both sides. It is possible, however (in fact desirable), to express differing opinions in the early stages. If people are not allowed to express their opinions on the front end of a discussion about a new service, be assured they will express them later at a less appropriate time.[8]

2. Some members will leave. Don't think that by avoiding controversy (such as the controversy created by introducing a new service) you will avoid the loss of disenchanted members. David DeSelm, in the video *A Church for the Twenty-First Century,* observes that "you're going to lose people even if you *don't* change."[9] He's right. You will lose dissatisfied members whether you add a new service or not. If you add the service, some folks from the right side of the bell curve will leave. If you don't, some visionaries from the left side will leave. The question is: Which dissatisfied members would you rather lose, the Never Adopters or the Innovators? If it is any consolation, it may be helpful to know that neither group will drop out of church life when they leave your congregation. The visionaries go to more progressive churches, the stalwarts to more traditional ones. The question is: Who would you rather keep?

3. The battle is for the Middle Adopters. You won't need to work very hard (if at all) to convince your Innovators and Early Adopters of the value of a new service. The Late Adopters will not be convinced before the new service actually becomes successful. But if you can convince the majority of Middle Adopters to support the initiative, you are on your way.

Remember, Middle Adopters are more easily swayed by Late Adopters than Early Adopters. Most Middle Adopters, while good and reasonable people, prefer the known to the unknown, the present certainty to the future's uncertainty. This does not mean Middle Adopters are closed to reason or cannot catch the excitement of a new vision. They're just normal people with normal fears of the unknown. As Malphurs observes, the majority of these people "tend to vote for the status quo unless they are given a good reason to change, or are assured that change will not result in a loss of quality."[10]

4. Make Early Adopters your allies. Generally, Early Adopters are well respected in the church. (Innovators often are not.) Their words are given serious consideration and their leadership is usually followed. First make a list of who these people are. Then solicit their active support. Ask them to endorse the new service in formal meetings and informal discussions. Explain that it is often conversations in the halls and on the telephone that influence Middle Adopters more than anything else. And in board and committee meetings let them know that it will be their support that may make the difference between success and failure.

Develop a Strategy of Diffusion

"A wise leader," observes Doug Murren, "will subscribe to a basic three-step process in presenting new directions to the church: (1) explain the idea to the core group, (2) collaborate with the committed workers, and (3) share with the entire congregation."[11] I have observed enough casualties of churches trying to add a new service to justify mentioning what should be obvious: Start at the top. Your primary church leadership body (session, board, church council, vestry) should be the first to formally receive your proposal. Don't start with the worship committee, your small group, finance board, or other organization in the church. There are two reasons:

1. If you formally present the idea to some other group or committee first, and members of the leadership body learn about it secondhand, you lose your ability to control the presentation of the idea and your ability to respond to questions that will invariably arise.
2. If members of the leadership body hear about the idea of a new service through secondhand conversation, you will create resistance if and when the idea comes before that group. Many will resist the proposal simply because they were not the first to be informed.

Figure 14

Diffusion Sequence for Introducing the New Service Idea

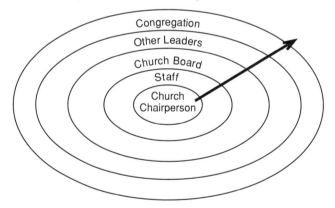

Figure 14 illustrates the appropriate diffusion of a new idea through the layers of bureaucracy of the church. Leith Anderson writes: "Most organizations have layers of opinion makers, informally ranked in concentric circles of increasing size. Begin with the . . . men and women in the inner circle. Once they are agreed on change, move to the next circle and then the next circle until the whole organization has ownership."[12]

Layer 1: Church Chairperson

It is important to recruit the president of the church or chairperson of the board as one of your early allies. During the coming months the times and places in which this person will have the opportunity to affirm the idea of a new service make it well worth your while to be sure he or she is supportive. Even if the person is not a significant opinion maker, the position demands your early consultation. The recommendations later in this chapter for generating support among lay leaders apply particularly to this one individual.

Layer 2: Staff

It is important for the church staff to present a single voice of support for the new service. If you have full- or part-time ministerial staff, share your personal conviction about a new style service with them early in the process. Take them with you on visits to churches that have successfully added a new style service. If these churches have positions comparable to that of your staff, have their staff discuss with your staff areas of common interest related to the new service.

In many churches the greatest challenge to staff unanimity comes from the full-time music director. If the proposed service is a contemporary service in addition to an existing traditional service, and if your music director is schooled in the fine arts of the historic music of the church, he or she may resist the new service. Village Baptist Church (Beaverton, Oreg.) concluded that after years of providing one style of service, it had an opportunity to broaden its ministry through the addition of a more contemporary service. The church's music director had a degree in classical music and was an accomplished musician. But he soon realized, to his credit, that the music that would be necessary to provide an attractive service in the contemporary hour was neither of his genre nor his taste. When the church called a young man from a church in southern Oregon to coordinate the music in the contemporary service, the music director was supportive, even as the church added a second contemporary service due to the popular response. As the music director told me, "I still, for the life of me, can't understand what people see in that kind of music. But if that's what it takes to get them to church, I'm not going to stand in the way." (In a conversation with the pastor a few months ago, however, I was told that the music director has since left to go to a church that more closely shares his musical values.) Hopefully your music director is able to model the qualities of a disciple committed to reaching people, even if he or she may not be the one to ultimately lead the people in this area.

Layer 3: Church Board

One of the most critical steps to seeing your church implement a new service is convincing the leadership board to not only adopt the idea but actively support it. The following suggestions grow out of conversations with pastors who have succeeded—and some who have failed—in soliciting the support of their church board. You may wish to modify these suggestions based on your situation. But I encourage you to take seriously the process of board adoption.

Before the Board Meeting

Before the meeting in which you first introduce the idea of a new service, make the following preparations:

1. *Meet with each board member (or couple) individually and informally.* Meet with each member over lunch; in your home or at a restaurant are ideal places. Begin with the church president or board chairperson. Share your personal convictions about the idea, and your personal journey to this point. Ask each person you meet with to pray about the idea, looking to God for his will to be made known. Also ask each person to list any questions that come to mind about the idea of a new service, and to let you know

71

what those questions are before the meeting in which the idea will be introduced.

Encourage those who share your enthusiasm for a new style service to be supportive in the upcoming board meeting, as well as in any subsequent meetings or private conversations. Your goal is to solicit as much informal support for the initiative as possible prior to the meeting. This may sound like Washington-style politics with the president lobbying members of Congress for support. Perhaps it is. But just because an idea is inspired doesn't mean it will be accepted.

Ask members not to discuss the proposal prior to the board meeting. Explain that your plan is to present the idea first to church leadership, of which they are a part, before any further plans or commitments are made. If there are other "gatekeepers" in your church who may not be on the official leadership board but have informal veto power, add them to your informal meetings list and endeavor to solicit their support.

2. Talk with pastors who have experience in adding a new service. It will be easier to describe the benefits of adding a new service if you have firsthand knowledge of churches that have successfully done so and are now reaping those same benefits. Finding such churches may take some research, but it can provide a powerful argument in favor of taking similar steps, particularly if these churches are of your denomination or theological persuasion. Talking with pastors who have "been there and done that" will also help you be aware of the pitfalls.

Rev. Doug Samples, senior pastor of Bakersfield First Church of the Nazarene (Bakersfield, Calif.), researched dozens of other Nazarene churches that had already added a new service. He wrote letters and made numerous phone calls to pastors, soliciting their advice. Here are a few insights from his collection of conversations, which he was kind enough to share with me:

- "The planning stage for the new service should be at least six months. Publicity should begin six weeks before the first service." *Pastor, Kansas City (Mo.) First Nazarene Church*

- "Offer additional Sunday school classes Sunday evening if the new service will be Sunday evening. Don't make Sunday morning (or Sunday evening) the only option for classes." *Executive, Nazarene Headquarters, Division of Sunday School Ministries*

- "Don't attempt to divide the present congregation; rather, launch a new service with primarily new people." *Pastor, Porterville (Calif.) Nazarene Church*

- "Begin the new service in a natural 'up time' (Christmas, fall, Easter, etc.) and run for a six-month trial period. Use two different sets of ushers and greeters. Don't try to divide existing Sunday school classes, start new ones." *Pastor, Dinuba (Calif.) Nazarene Church*

- "Two services will be successful, but require a great deal more planning. Be sure people know why you are doing this." *Pastor, San Luis Obispo (Calif.) Nazarene Church*

- "Try to anticipate impact on Sunday school. We lost thirty people in adding the new service, but after adding new classes attendance is now up by six." *Pastor, Donson Ranch Nazarene Church, Chandler (Ariz.)*

- "How full the sanctuary is before beginning is important. Church now has three services and three Sunday Schools. The ideal time to start is fall." *Pastor, Mesa (Ariz.) Nazarene Church*

- "Total increase when new service was added: three hundred. Use different worship leader but same preacher/message. Some at the traditional service were disturbed because so many started attending the contemporary service." *Pastor, Visalia (Calif.) Nazarene Church*

If you are part of a denominational family, ask your regional or national office for a list of some churches that have added a new style service and are reaching new people as a result. Presenting three or four examples of churches within your own church family that have successfully added a new service will be a partial response to those who may worry about whether a new service will compromise the theology or identity of the church.

Visit a church in your area that offers multiple service styles. Then later in the week talk with the pastor. (Remember to take staff members with you.) Focus on how that church first introduced the idea of a new service to the leaders and congregation. Learn enough about the church to speak knowledgeably about it when you discuss the idea with your own leaders.

3. Write down the questions people will ask about the new service. The questions you encounter will fall into one of two categories: macroissues and microissues. Macroissues will relate to purpose, strategy, and priorities of the new service. Questions might include: Why are we doing this? When would it happen? Is it consistent with our purpose? Will it be different from the present service?

Microissues, on the other hand, focus on questions of tactics and specifics of implementation, such as: What time would the new service begin? When will we have Sunday school? Where do we find musicians? Would the choir sing in both services?

Don't attempt to anticipate or answer all the microissues that may arise. That is not even your task at this point. But do be clear on the macroissues and your response to these questions.

After you have written down each question, write the answer that you believe best responds to each question. Do not distribute this at the meeting, but it will help you anticipate the questions and be prepared with a thoughtful response. At the end of this chapter I have listed some macroquestions that are commonly asked by laypeople. Develop answers to these questions that you feel accurately represent your convictions.

4. Prepare handouts for presenting the proposal. Below is a list of suggested handouts and their contents. I recommend that you distribute the material as three separate handouts during the meeting. This will focus the group's attention on each specific topic and not tempt members to skim through other pages ahead of time.

Handout 1

A. *The Church's Mission Statement.* If your church has a mission statement, print it on a sheet of paper and distribute it to each board member. As noted earlier, the new service should be presented as a natural outgrowth of your church's reason for existence. If there will be people at the meeting who participated in the development of the mission statement, solicit their support of a new service as a tangible outgrowth of their work in the formulation of the church's mission.

Handout 2

B. *Statistics on the church's five- and ten-year worship attendance history.* Many times church members, particularly in a slowly declining church, have not seen the current attendance in the context of a long-term trend. A graph of these statistics will increase their awareness for needed change in the status quo and can be helpful in projecting the future if current attendance patterns continue. Note the word *attendance,* not *membership.* Membership is not an accurate indicator of a church's health.[13]

C. *The average number of visitors over the past five years.* Since no one joins a church without first visiting, a church's growth potential is directly related to the number of visitors that come through the doors. Research indicates that growth in worship attendance requires that at least 5 percent of a morning service be first- or second-time visitors from the surrounding community.[14] Compare your church's visitor percentage against this point of reference. One compelling reason for the addition of a new service is to increase the number of visitors.

Handout 3

D. *The proposal.* Describe the new service proposal that you wish the board to consider. Present the ideas you have about the kind of service it should be and the kind of people you believe God is calling the church to reach. But keep your options open on specific issues. The board's response will most likely be to authorize you to select an exploratory task force to bring back a report and/or recommendation.[15]

E. *Reasons for a new service.* Review the material from chapter 1 and add any other reasons for a new service that are appropriate for your church. One or two sentences for each reason is adequate. During your presentation you will elabo-

75

rate on each reason, so prepare some notes prior to the meeting.

The Board Meeting

I encourage you to call a special meeting to present and discuss the proposal of a new service. Most board members will know the purpose of the meeting, since you already will have discussed the idea with each of them individually. A special meeting emphasizes the importance of the initiative and frees you from the pressure of other agenda issues.

Begin with an affirmation of your personal commitment to your church, and the joy you have in ministering to the congregation. Share your intent of staying with the church indefinitely (if true) to help the church move forward in reaching the great potential you believe God has given the church in your community.

Distribute a copy of the church's mission statement (handout 1) and review it, along with how and when it was developed. Affirm those who were involved in the process and share your desire to see that purpose actualized in tangible ways.

Whether or not you have a mission statement, review your understanding of God's purpose in sending Christ to earth, and the conviction about the important role your congregation has in carrying out that mission.

Distribute and discuss graphs of the church's recent worship attendance and visitor history (handout 2). Include in your discussion the question, Where will our present course take us? When Charles Laird became the new pastor of Westminster Presbyterian Church (Duluth, Minn.), he developed a chart of the church's recent membership decline and extended two dotted lines from the present into the future: one if the church's decline were to continue, and a second if the church were to experience 10 percent growth each year. (This chart is reviewed regularly in leadership and congregational sessions when Laird presents new directions for the church.)

Distribute the sheet describing the proposal and reasons for the new service (handout 3). Explain that you would like to present

76

an idea that you believe has exciting implications for the church, and why it merits the group's serious consideration.

As you present the idea of a new service, try to keep a balance between (1) communicating your passion and conviction that this is an important issue for the future of this church and (2) being open-minded to suggestions and enhancements so board members can develop ownership of the vision. A pastor friend of mine in Columbus, Ohio, told me he uses the phrase "Here's what we're thinking" when introducing a new idea to his leaders, while still encouraging their input.

Communicate why you believe a new service is an appropriate and necessary step for the church. Describe your personal pilgrimage in arriving at your position. Share the weeks or months of prayer you have devoted to seeking God's will, your commitment to see the church be most effective in ministry, your analysis of the church's trends, your discussions with other pastors, and your visits to other churches.

As you present the vision, focus on the potential increase in ministry and changed lives the service could bring. Be enthusiastic. If leaders believe you are eager to move ahead, they will be more inclined to support you (or less inclined to resist).

Remember to stress that the proposed change is an addition, not a substitution. Adding a new service is intended to reach a new group of people. It is not intended to force those who are happily attending the existing service(s) to accept anything new or different.

A second important part of your proposal should focus on the fact that the new service is a short-term experiment, not a long-term commitment. If the idea were to be accepted by the board, you would be looking at a four- to six-months trial. At that time the results of the new service would be reviewed and a recommendation made concerning its future. If the new service seems to be accomplishing the goal of touching a larger number of people with God's love, hopefully the board would decide to continue. If the goal is not being reached, however, appropriate action would also be recommended.

Before you conclude your presentation and entertain questions, revisit the list of reasons for a new service, and the value and unique benefits it could bring. Close with any additional comments relevant to your particular church.

Then open the meeting to discussion. Invite board members to respond, ask questions, offer suggestions. If possible, call first on respected leaders who you know support the idea. This sets the stage for a positive, proactive discussion. (Also try to conclude the discussion with respected people who support the idea.)

During the discussion keep in mind that a new service must eventually be the church's vision, not just the pastor's. Be open to all suggestions that may improve the outcome. However, don't present the proposal as a detached bystander with no interest in whether it is passed. Present it as a direction in which you believe God is calling the church, a direction in which you're prepared to lead.

Suggest that the goal of this meeting is not to make a decision. The purpose is simply to introduce the idea of a new service, present why it is an important part of the church's future ministry, and give individuals the information necessary to pray intelligently about it in the coming weeks.

Lyle Schaller suggests that throughout a group discussion on adding a new service, it may be necessary for the leader to occasionally redirect the group's attention to the question, What is the primary objective in our Sunday morning schedule? "To create a sense of unity? To increase the number of people attending worship? To offer choices to people? To reach potential new members? To fill a partially empty building? To offer as many persons as feasible an opportunity for a meaningful worship experience? To avoid overworking the minister? To minimize the burden on lay volunteers who sing in the choir or serve as ushers? To open up more opportunities for active participation by more people? To reach as many young parents as possible? To encourage everyone to attend both worship and a Sunday School class?"[16]

Schaller goes on to suggest: "After these objectives have been defined and listed in order of importance, and that set of priorities has been agreed to, it will be relatively easy to decide whether

78

the primary objectives are most likely to be fulfilled by scheduling only one worship service or by planning for two. It is essential, however, that the objectives be arranged in order of importance. Rarely is it possible to achieve all the desired objectives."[17]

Write down questions raised about a new service, since similar questions will come up at each point in the diffusion process (other committee meetings, meetings with teachers and officers, congregational meetings). If possible, encourage others in the group who support the idea to respond to questions. Encourage dialogue among the group, not just questions and answers to and from you. This will avoid the impression that you are the only one in favor of the idea.

Don't get defensive. Encourage questions and enhancements. An important goal of the meeting is to see church leaders move toward ownership, not just acceptance. Positively present a new style worship service as an appropriate and strategic step into the future, and ask members to identify issues that are important for success.

The discussion should be concluded by encouraging members to make this a matter for serious personal prayer in the coming days. Note that while you may be convinced of God's leading in this direction, it would be highly unlikely for the church to successfully move forward on this idea unless church leaders are as well.

Set a date for the next meeting, at which time you would hope for a final decision on the proposal. If an exploratory task force is appointed, give those on the task force several months to complete their work. Reaffirm your personal support for the idea of a new service prior to closing. Let members know that you would be pleased to discuss the idea personally with any of them prior to the next meeting. Stress that you do not intend to push this idea any farther if the board is not entirely supportive.

The Second Board Meeting

Prior to the next board meeting, in which the vote will be taken on the new service, contact each member of the board personally and ask whether any questions have come to mind. Consider how those questions might be answered and prepare any material that would support your response and clarify the issue. If any questions from the board members affect a particular staff member (music minister, Christian education director, youth minister), brief him or her on the issue and discuss possible responses to the question or problem. Be sure all staff members are at the meeting, and during the question-answer session, invite the staff to respond to the questions.

Don't feel that all the issues must be resolved at this meeting. Some questions (such as scheduling, Sunday school class conflicts, finding musical talent) can be answered only as you begin to research and plan the new service. But these are issues of how to start a new service, not whether to start one. The purpose of this meeting is to obtain from church leadership a concerted vote of confidence—a green light to move forward on a new style service.

As in the previous meeting, if you know there are certain Early Adopters who are well respected and supportive of the proposal, give them early exposure in the discussion. If you are friends with the pastor of a church that has successfully started a new service, consider inviting this person to the meeting as a voice of positive experience. If the church is of your denomination, so much the better.

Assuming the board approves the new service, send a personal follow-up note to each board member immediately after the meeting. Note their personal support or concern regarding a new service and express your optimism for the future of the church through this faithful move toward expanded ministry. In the letter, affirm your personal commitment to make the new service a priority, but not at the expense of compromising the quality of the present service(s). Ask for their support of the new service in their conversations with others, since their role as leaders is important. If they are on other committees or in Sunday school classes in which the new service may be discussed, ask that they be supportive ambassadors for the board and its decision.

Suggest that a churchwide leadership meeting be called to introduce the idea of a new service to all elected, appointed, and volunteer leaders. If it is possible within your church constitution, don't present the idea of a new service for a congregational vote. Leaders of growing churches seldom take growth initiatives to their membership for approval. To do so runs the significant risk of asking the majority (the Middle Adopters) to serve as visionaries. They can't. And they won't. Rather, position the new service as a short-term commitment that the leaders have determined is an important step for the church to take in the pursuit of its mission and purpose. The goal of the meeting is to present the vision and explain the next steps in the process.

Whenever possible, from this time on, refer to the new service initiative as a decision that is supported (hopefully unanimously) by the church board. The assumption behind the existence of a church board is that it represents and speaks for the congregation.

Layer 4: Other Leaders

The same week you receive board approval, send a personalized letter to church members who hold elected, appointed, or volunteer positions in the church. Identify people who serve on committees and task forces, Sunday school teachers and officers, small group leaders, day school staff, and so on. Invite them to attend an upcoming church leaders' meeting in two to three weeks to learn about an important new development in the church's ministry.

In the letter explain that this invitation is being extended only to those who have responsibilities in the church and who are leaders and key members of the congregation. (That is, make them feel special about being invited.) Explain the board's recent vote to initiate an enlarged outreach strategy in the form of a new style worship service, and that the purpose of the meeting is to share and expand this new vision with church leaders. Do not communicate or imply that the purpose of this meeting is to take a vote or ask for approval. "If possible, avoid voting," says Don Brandt, a Lutheran consultant who has helped churches begin a new service. "Votes involve winners and losers."[18] The purpose of the meeting is to introduce the idea of a new service, answer questions, and encourage suggestions about how to make the new service most effective for reaching newcomers.

In preparation for this leadership meeting, prepare a handout for each person who will attend. Include similar information as was distributed in the church board meeting. If there was a final resolution passed by the board, include that as well.

In addition, prepare a list of questions and answers about the new service. A sample of a handout developed by First Nazarene Church (Pasadena, Calif.) is included in appendix B. These documents can be stapled together for distribution at the meeting.

If the chairperson of the church board is eloquent and a strong supporter of the new service, let him or her chair the meeting. Of course, you and the church staff should actively participate. But having a respected lay leader chair the meeting will strengthen its impact and reinforce the support of a cross section of church leadership.

Prior to this lay leadership meeting encourage several respected Early Adopters to voice their support early in the meeting. Explain to them that such comments will be helpful in setting a positive mood for the entire discussion.

Part of the presentation to these leaders should be to summarize the steps that will be taken in moving toward the new service. The following eight steps summarize the sequence leading to a successful new service. (The remainder of this book enlarges on these areas.)

Step 1: Identifying the target audience
Step 2: Defining the goal of the new service
Step 3: Identifying appropriate themes
Step 4: Designing the service
Step 5: Determining a time and place to meet
Step 6: Promoting and publicizing the new service
Step 7: Following up with visitors and prospects
Step 8: Evaluating the service

The approximate time when the first new service will be held should also be mentioned, but stress that it is only a tentative target and that the actual date will be set by the planning committee once it feels it has completed each step.

Most churches find that seven to nine months are required to effectively and successfully plan, prepare for, and promote a new style service. Based on my observations, I would strongly encourage you to set a start date for the new service no sooner than six months after your planning team is assembled.

In the lay leadership meeting explain that this is an experiment and that approximately four to six months after the first service there will be an evaluation of whether the new service has realized its hopes and goals. Also emphasize that the existing service(s) in the church will not be affected. Explain that the intent of the new service is to focus on those people *not* attending the church. Many of the guidelines for introducing the new service to the church board should be followed in this meeting as well. And recall also the principles of change presented at the beginning of this chapter.

Handle the question-answer segment of the meeting in much the same way as in the church board meeting.

Layer 5: Congregation

Doug Samples has observed that "congregational acceptance and support will be the greatest challenge you face. Resistance to change will surface, especially when traditions are broken."[19] A few churches will buy into the idea quickly. In most churches, however, a strategy will be required to assure success.

The most important fact to remember when communicating to the congregation is this: The church board and leaders have already endorsed the idea of starting a new service. Pastor Steve Green, describing the church's recent board meeting in a letter to the congregation, wrote, "In that evening, your church board, on two different occasions, voted unanimously to move our congregation to a multiple-worship option."[20]

Your Middle Adopters will be more inclined to support the idea if respected church leaders support it. For this reason, use all opportunities to drop names of those who have voiced support, and don't hesitate to use your allies to bring the silent majority on board. Once the Middle Adopters have determined that a new service is acceptable, the Late Adopters will follow. They won't always follow quietly, but they will follow. I like the way a Nazarene pastor in Columbus introduces a new idea to his people. He says, "Not many pastors are lucky enough to have people like you who will allow change."

A second important part of your congregational strategy should focus on the fact that this is a short-term experiment, not a long-term commitment. Ask members to reserve judgment during the trial period for the new service and to withhold negative comments until a time when the experiment will be evaluated. Then they will be free to share their opinions and will be guaranteed an audience of serious listeners.

Here are some additional suggestions for building support in the larger congregation prior to beginning the new service:

Lay testimonies. The fact is that sometimes a layperson will be more believable to another church member than a pastor or staff member. Therefore it may be helpful to have a lay leader give a report to the congregation concerning the new service initiative and the endorsement of the leadership council.

A congregational survey. "People feel better when their opinions have been sought in advance of any decision being made," observes Mundey.[21] In helping churches add a new service, I have been fascinated by the consistently high percentage of members who answer positively to a survey querying their attitude toward a new service. A good survey can serve several purposes. It can (1) assess the attitude of members toward the present service, (2) evaluate their openness to a new service, (3) identify people groups that members desire to reach, (4) legitimize the idea of a new service through widespread endorsement from the congregation.

Printed questions and answers. Develop a printed question-answer sheet that speaks to the issues members previously have raised. This indicates the sincerity with which you take their concerns, and also helps reinforce the purpose of the new service in the minds of members.

Multimedia about your target audience. To build a sense of expectancy and vision for outreach, you may find it helpful to develop a quality slide or video presentation that focuses on the target audience you wish to reach through the new service. If there are skilled media producers in your church, it would be an enjoyable project for them to develop a five-to-seven-minute, upbeat media piece that highlights the need to reach this people group. The piece might include interviews or comments from people in this group about their sense of hopelessness, their desires, their problems, their attitudes toward traditional church, their belief in God, and so on. It could include charts and graphs showing the number of people in this category around your church and the number who attend a church. A well-produced presentation will speak to people's emotions, and enhance your intellectual appeal with feelings from the heart.

A report on research. Over time, as your worship planning team gathers information on the target group, share it with your members. Use bulletin inserts, pulpit interviews, and newsletter articles by laity to keep the congregation informed.

Between the first public announcement and the first new service, keep the purpose of the church in front of people. Ultimately the only reason for a new service is to pursue the church's mission. Regularly review and highlight that mission statement. Some churches put their mission statement in the bulletin every Sunday. Others design banners that reflect it. Refer to your mission statement when new members are welcomed into the fellowship. Integrate it into sermons and prayers. Review it in church board and committee meetings. The more people are conscious of—and supportive of—the church's reason for being, the more open they will be to new ways of accomplishing that mission.

Your "Sales Objective"

In "selling" the idea of a new service to the congregation, your goal is to see members fall into one of four categories:

1. Involvement. Ideally, there are some who will prepare for, plan, promote, and participate in the new service. There will be numerous opportunities for people to get involved in activities related to the new service, or they may simply agree to attend regularly and invite friends. Your new-service planning team will want to provide as many opportunities as possible for people to have a part in the process.

But not everyone can or will directly participate in the new service. For those who don't, your "sales objective" is support.

2. Support. Your goal for those not directly involved in the new service is to gain their endorsement of the new venture. They may not attend the new service, but they support the church moving in this direction. If you can get a significant number of members, particularly leaders, to support the new service, it's money in the bank!

Support implies active endorsement, however. And not everyone in the church will be able to bring themselves to take such a proactive stance. For those who can't, your "sales objective" is acceptance.

3. Acceptance. Whereas support is active endorsement, acceptance is passive endorsement. Those who are willing to accept the decision of church leadership to move forward with a new service respect the knowledge of the leaders and the system of church government. If the board has voted in favor of the new service, they are willing to accept it. While they may not be strong advocates, neither will they be adversaries.

Still, some good folks in the church simply won't be able to see the reason for a new service. In fact, they are rather certain there is no good reason. For those people, your "sales objective" is tolerance.

4. Tolerance. Despite their sincere commitment to Christ and the church, some will simply not be able to support the idea of a new service. It is beyond their paradigm to grasp the possibility that a new service could be necessary. Your goal with these people is to simply buy time. Here will be one of the great benefits of presenting the new service as an experiment. Ask for their commitment to withhold negative comments until there has been adequate time to try the idea. At some point in the future they will be encouraged to share their opinions, and they will be heard.

There is a relationship between how people respond to a new idea (see fig. 13) and your "sales objectives" for each group. Figure 15 presents your goals.

Figure 15

What Kind of Response Are You Seeking?

Church Members		"Sales Objective"
Innovators	——→	Involvement
Early Adopters	——→	Support
Middle Adopters	——→	Acceptance
Late Adopters	——→	Tolerance

Concerns Before a New Service Begins

Here is a list of concerns you will encounter regarding a new style service. It will be helpful for you to spend time in prayer, Bible study, and research to arrive at responses to these issues. I have given a few abbreviated responses that you may use or adapt, but eventually you will need to develop responses that accurately reflect your own convictions.

Lay Concerns	Possible Responses
We won't know everyone.	Is "knowing everyone" the primary purpose of our church? Most people won't know more than forty-five to fifty people in a church, regardless of the church's size or number of services. The benefit one receives in the worship service is not dependent on how many people he or she knows.

87

Lay Concerns	Possible Responses
We will become two churches.	Two churches can reach more people than one church. What's wrong with starting a new church? We will be reaching people through our "second" church that would not come to our "first" church.
It will stretch our leaders too thin.	Perhaps they need to cut back or delegate in other areas. This is an opportunity to involve more members. More in attendance will mean more income, which will allow us to hire more staff.
They can come to our present service.	They haven't been. Is there any indication they are beginning to or ever will? Spiritual pilgrims are not at the same point in their journey as members. Would you go to a church for very long if you did not understand the language?

Concerns After a New Service Begins

After a new service has been successfully established, the questions are not over; they will simply change. Here are some issues and/or concerns you may encounter sometime after the new service begins.

Lay Concerns	Possible Responses
It isn't "real" church.	What is "real" church, and how do you know? Can people only meet God in one kind of service? They need time to grow in their faith.

Lay Concerns	Possible Responses
The music isn't Christ honoring.	Charles Wesley and Martin Luther wrote many hymns to the tune of songs sung in local taverns. Must Christ-honoring music be slow? Let's look at the words that are being sung.
That service is growing too fast.	Do you feel that you are losing authority in the church? Total attendance is growing for the first time in years; isn't that wonderful? We seem to have touched a need in people's lives, haven't we?
The pastor is more interested in the new service and new people.	Why do you think so? What do you think Jesus was saying in the parable of the lost sheep, the lost coin, and the lost son? Perhaps we need an additional staff person for calling on members who feel neglected.

In Conclusion

Different churches will present different challenges in terms of winning support for a new service. As a rule, the longer a church has gone without the addition of a new service, the more challenging it will be to add one. At the same time, it is usually these churches that need a new service the most. Yet even if you are in a church that seems open to change and willing to grow, it is important to spend careful and prayerful attention to getting your leaders on board. Once you lay this solid foundation of support for the new service, you have a body moving in concert rather than single parts in isolation. These efforts will greatly increase the chances of your new service being a success.

What Kind of Service Do You Want?

Some years ago a popular Hollywood movie illustrated an important church growth principle. In *Field of Dreams,* a young man had a strange, recurring vision of building a baseball diamond in his cornfield. A voice kept telling him, "If you build it, they will come!" The young man eventually built his ball field. And indeed his dream did come true.

The same holds true in the church: Build the number and variety of programs before it seems necessary. New programs precede growth; they do not follow it. If your church is not growing, and has not for the past five years, simply working harder at doing what you have been doing will not result in new growth. You must begin acting like the church you want to become, applying the biblical principle of acting on faith.

One of the most strategic areas for such new programming is beginning a new style service. When you start a new service, you are programming for new growth, and you will begin reaching new people.

So who are the new people you will be reaching?

Define Your Target Audience

Earlier we suggested a model to describe the constituency of your present worship service. To refresh your memory see figure 16.

Figure 16

To Whom Is Your Present Service Most Attractive?

	Generational Group		
	Baby Busters (born 1965–78)	Baby Boomers (born 1946–64)	Seniors (born before 1946)
Christian			
Seeker			

(Spiritual Condition)

This model identifies two axes along which most churches can define the constituents of their present service—*generational group* and *spiritual condition*. Of the six possibilities identified in this grid, 96 percent of all church services in America focus on either Baby Boomer Christians or Senior Christians. Of course, in one church service there will be some generational overlap due to personal tastes, church loyalty, convenient scheduling, friendships, location, and pastor loyalty. But particularly when newcomers are analyzed, most churches find that their target groups fall into one of these two categories. Having a primary target group is neither good nor bad. It just is.

It is necessary to understand your primary constituency before you think about a different group on which to focus your new service.

Before considering the possible target groups for a new service, one additional variable needs to be added to the above model—*cultural identity*. That is, what (if any) ethnic identification will your new target audience reflect?

Let's consider each of these three variables—generational group, spiritual condition, cultural identity—which will be used to define your target audience.

Generational Group

Sociologists and demographers tell us that the American population is composed of three distinct generational groups, each with its own unique identity, behavior, and predictable characteristics: Baby Busters, Baby Boomers, and Seniors.[1]

While certainly every person is unique in his or her own respect, there is adequate research to support the thesis that people in a particular generational group share an extraordinary number of attitudes and behavior patterns with others in that same group; attitudes and behavior patterns that are distinctly different from either of the two other groups.

Below is a table, originally printed in the *LifeLine* newsletter,[2] that outlines some of the more notable characteristics of each of these three generational groups:

Baby Busters	Baby Boomers	Seniors
Hazy sense of their own identity	Relate to individual goals	Loyal to societal institutions
Quirky individualism	Well-educated generation	Believe that people serve institutions
Desire personal freedom, autonomy	"Not enough time"	Relate to group goals
"Indifferent" generation	Desire and search for meaning	Communal ethics
Interests more important than work	Value security	Finances focused on savings
	Value affluence	

93

Baby Busters	Baby Boomers	Seniors
Cynical, disillusioned, skeptical	Appreciate free and open expression	Standardization is valued
"Have-nots"	Distrust organizational institutions	Resist change
Slow to grow up	Not motivated by guilt	Much religious heritage
Materialism outwardly rejected	Given to self-analysis, questioning, comparing	Willing to sacrifice self-interest for group benefit
Hopeless, hurt-filled	Pragmatic	Motivated by responsibility and duty
Lonely		"Do the best you can with what you've got"

Below are a few descriptive paragraphs on each of these three generational groups. There are many excellent books available that explore the unique qualities and characteristics of each of these groups. I strongly encourage you to read several such books about the generational group on which you plan to focus your new service.

Seniors

Gerontologist Ken Dychtwald notes that America is rapidly graying. Since 1900, life expectancy has increased by twenty-eight years. Two thirds of all those who have ever lived to age sixty-five are alive today.[3] During the next ten to twenty years the "age wave" will become one of the most significant forces affecting American society. Successful ministry and outreach to this generation of older adults is not by any means an easy task for today's churches. In fact, there are some experts who say it is perhaps the most difficult generation to reach. Figure 17 reports on one study that typifies others, indicating that

Figure 17

Age at Conversion

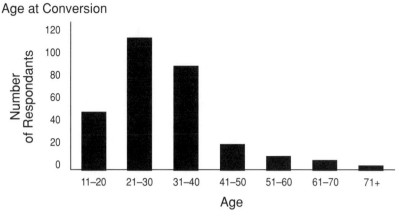

churches are not particularly successful in evangelizing older adults.[4]

Many of today's senior citizens are far removed from the traditional stereotypes that society—and the church—hold about them. Comparing today's senior adults with previous generations, *U.S. News and World Report* says, "What is important about this new generation is its difference not only in size, but in vitality and outlook."[5]

Win Arn goes so far as to create a new phrase describing many of today's older adults. He calls them "New Seniors." Arn identifies their characteristics and suggests that the senior adult ministry strategy of most churches today is woefully lacking in reaching this group. New Seniors:

- do not think of themselves as old;
- have goals they want to accomplish;
- enjoy going out;
- look forward to the future;
- have supportive friendships;
- are often part of a group that shares a common interest;
- view retirement as a time for work, study, service, and play.[6]

Helpful books about this age category include:

Arn, Win, and Charles Arn. *Catch the Age Wave.* Grand Rapids: Baker, 1994.

Arn, Win, and Charles Arn. *Live Long and Love It!* Wheaton: Tyndale House, 1993.

Dychtwald, Ken. *Age Wave.* New York: Bantam Books, 1992.

Wirt, Sherwood. *I Don't Know What Old Is, But Old Is Older Than Me!* Nashville: Thomas Nelson, 1994.

Wolfe, David. *Serving the Ageless Market.* New York: McGraw Hill, 1991.

Baby Boomers

Of the three generations that compose the American adult population, Baby Boomers have received the most publicity. One reason is that despite the fact that Baby Boomers were born in a time span of only eighteen years, they compose fully one third of the American population. "From the time of its arrival, the baby boom has strongly affected American society," says Landon Jones. "At every stage in their lives the baby boomers change the nature of the life stage they enter, and force the nation to devote extra-ordinary attention to the problems and needs of people in that age group."[7]

Another reason Baby Boomers have attracted so much attention, from sociologists as well as church leaders, is the characteristics that distinguish them from their parents. Robert Bast identifies some of the commonly accepted characteristics of this generation:

> *High expectations.* The relative wealth of their parents, and their own higher education, gave them a perspective on what they wanted, which was more than previous generations.
>
> *The psychology of affluence.* Baby Boomers assume that the continual accumulation of possessions is both possible and desirable. Acquiring more of everything is a matter of personal entitlement rather than a mere hope or dream.

96

Emotional expressiveness. They believe in giving free and open expression to one's emotions, with a priority on sincerity and honesty in human interaction. They despise hypocrisy and respect genuineness.

Individualism. Baby Boomers reject labels of any kind. They have little use for titles and prefer first names in all contexts. They have little brand loyalty, prefer not to identify with any political party, and are strongly committed to freedom of choice.

Distrust of institutions. They operate with an anti-institutional bias. Organized religion represents one of the least trusted of all institutions.[8]

Helpful books about this age group include:

Bast, Bob. *The Missing Generation.* Monrovia, Calif.: Church Growth Press, 1991.

Light, Paul. *Baby Boomers.* New York: Norton, 1988.

Murren, Doug. *The Baby Boomerang.* Ventura, Calif.: Regal, 1990.

Roof, Wade. *A Generation of Seekers.* San Francisco: Harper SanFrancisco, 1993.

Baby Busters

Called "Baby Busters" because of the considerable drop (bust) in the number of births after the baby boom, this age group is only now beginning to take on characteristics that are predictable. One pattern of this group, ironically, is the value they place in being unpredictable, and the desire to define themselves as different from Baby Boomers.

Some of the predominant characteristics of the Baby Buster generation include:

Freedom. Many Baby Busters reject the workaholism that often characterized their Baby Boomer parents as they sought to climb the corporate ladder. Flexibility, work-free weekends, and short-term tasks are valued by Baby Busters in regard to their occupation.

Helplessness and resentment. National and global issues such as world hunger, homelessness, AIDS, poverty, and pollution are so large that most Baby Busters feel helpless to do anything about them. Because these problems were "dumped" on them by previous generations, Baby Busters often feel resentful toward their predecessors.

Neglected. More than 40 percent of Baby Busters are children of divorce and nearly 50 percent lived in single-parent homes, usually headed by working mothers. As a result, sociologists suggest, many in this generation are very lonely.

Values rejection. Having observed what divorce, career climbing, and drug abuse have done to their parents, Baby Busters reject many of their parents' values and lifestyles. They appear to be more conservative and hold more traditional values. Many lack relational skills due to the broken and/or dysfunctional homes in which they grew up.

Postponing marriage and/or independence. Approximately 75 percent of young adults eighteen to twenty-four years old still live at home, the largest percentage since the Great Depression. Of men ages twenty-five to twenty-nine, 46 percent have never married, compared with only 19 percent of men in the same age bracket in 1970.[9]

Helpful books about this age category include:

Barna, George. *The Invisible Generation.* Glendale, Calif.: Barna Research Group, 1992.
Dunn, William. *The Baby Bust: A Generation Comes of Age.* Ithaca, N.Y.: American Demographics, 1993.
Gibb, Steven. *Twentysomething.* Chicago: Noble Press, 1991.
Sciacca, Fran. *Generation at Risk.* Chicago: Moody, 1991.

As you consider the generational group on whom you plan to focus your new service, realize that many areas of the service will be affected by your choice. Gary McIntosh suggests that while not every member of each generation sees things the same way, there are some potential areas of difficulty in generational attitudes toward worship:[10]

- *Pace*. Seniors like worship services to move along slowly and predictably. Baby Boomers like worship to move at a fast clip, and Baby Busters want it to move even quicker. Both Baby Boomers and Baby Busters look for some variety and spontaneity.
- *Lighting*. Seniors prefer softer lighting, as it gives more of a worshipful feeling. Baby Boomers and Baby Busters look for brighter lighting so they can see people well.
- *Sound*. Seniors appreciate being able to hear well but dislike sound that blasts. Baby Boomers want the sound louder but not intrusive. Baby Busters want the sound so loud they can feel it.
- *Length*. Seniors have a longer attention span and thus are willing to sit through longer services. The attention span of Baby Boomers is shorter, that of Baby Busters shorter still.
- *Formality*. Seniors expect a certain level of formality and decorum. Baby Boomers enjoy organization without the appearance of ritual. Baby Busters prefer a sense of spontaneity.
- *Participation*. Seniors tend to watch and enjoy. Churched Baby Boomers and Baby Busters want to participate, while unchurched Baby Boomers and Baby Busters prefer to be entertained.
- *Music*. Seniors love the hymnal and familiar songs of faith, with music slowly paced and reverent. Baby Boomers and Baby Busters like to "sing a new song" to the Lord.

Spiritual Condition

As I mentioned, the majority of church services in America are focused on Christians. While an increasing number of churches are trying to be "seeker friendly," and while some churches still include invitations to accept Christ, in reality pastors and service planners assume a predominantly Christian audience. And their assumption is correct.

The term *seeker service* has entered the vocabulary of an increasing number of pastors and church growth students. *Seeker-sensitive service* and *seeker-friendly service* are often used interchangeably. These two terms, however, should not be confused with *seeker-targeted service* or *seeker-driven service*. The first two terms describe a church service in which the assumption of the service planners is that a predominant number of attenders are Christians and are present for the purpose of worshiping God and enhancing their spiritual growth. The last two terms describe a service in which the assumption of the service planners is that a predominant number of attenders are non-Christians and are present for the purpose of evaluating God and enhancing their spiritual exploration.

Considering the spiritual condition of your target audience—specifically, their relationship to Christ—is an important step in defining your new service. A clear understanding of this issue and the assumptions you are making about your audience will be necessary before you can identify themes and topics that will make the service relevant and successful.

Believer Focused

The larger the church, the more difficult it is to plan a one-hour worship experience that is genuine and meaningful for everyone. That is because the larger your congregation, the more diverse the people and the spiritual journeys they bring to the experience. Some are single adults, while others are married; some are older adults, while others are young; some are new believers, while others have been Christians for fifty years or more.

But Christians are called to be transformed into one mind and heart—that of Jesus Christ. The common denominator of a believer-focused worship service is the assumption that those in attendance are there to worship God. A believer-focused service can and frequently will have unbelievers present. And it is certainly appropriate and increasingly necessary for churches to make their worship services seeker sensitive. But a service with a target audience of believers does not define its success on the basis of how many souls were saved in that service and how many unchurched people were in attendance.

"Worship is the adoration and praise of that which delights us," writes John Piper. "We praise what we enjoy, because praise completes the enjoyment. We worship God for the pleasure to be had in him."[11] Unchurched seekers cannot be expected to relate easily to such a goal.

Does this mean that a believer-focused service is exclusively for Christians? Not at all. In fact, many believer-focused services in growing churches attract unchurched people in fairly large numbers. Jack Hayford identifies four ways in which he seeks to make non-Christians feel they are a part of the service:

Invite them to relax. Before the service formally begins, he welcomes those in attendance and lets them know that this is a time in which they are not trying to impress God but simply trying to be themselves in the presence of God, since God knows who they are anyway.

Acknowledge their awkwardness. During the service the pastor will often acknowledge to newcomers that the particular style of worship used in the service may be new or unusual to some.

Encourage partial participation. Instead of making visitors do something unusual to them, the church will often encourage newcomers to participate in a way in which they feel comfortable, or reassure them that it is fine not to participate at all.

Explain the service as it progresses. From time to time the worship leader will explain the purpose and scriptural basis of a

101

particular part of the service. The music or the raised hands or the applause or the sermon or the testimonies in a service each have a purpose, which can be clarified for the benefit of members and nonmembers alike.[12]

A believer-focused service can have an evangelistic benefit as people experience the presence of God and God's people. But a believer-focused service is intended to bring Christian men and women into the presence of God and to see them leave as more complete persons.

Seeker Focused

In its basic form, the idea of a seeker-targeted service is not new. In the 1940s and 1950s many churches conducted evangelistic services on Sunday evening. The Sunday evening services in many churches today are the remnants of those evangelistic services, which over time lost their purpose and simply became poor clones of the Sunday morning service. The evangelistic rallies of Billy Sunday and Billy Graham were also seeker services of their day. In fact, John Wesley conducted seeker services throughout England, and his converts eventually became the Methodist Church.

While *worship service* is a legitimate and accurate term for a believer-focused service, some question whether the term is appropriate to describe a seeker-targeted service. Rev. Bill Hybels, pastor of Willow Creek Community Church (South Barrington, Ill.)—the church widely associated with popularizing the term *seeker service*—does not use the word worship to describe the church's weekend seeker services. The word is reserved for the midweek service for believers.

George Hunter studied a variety of churches that are growing through reaching unchurched people. In his excellent book *Church for the Unchurched* he describes these "apostolic churches" and identifies one of their common denominators: "I found that all the leaders of apostolic congregations . . . take their local culture(s) seriously; they all adapt to the target culture."[13]

102

"Each week," says Rev. Rick Warren, "we remind ourselves who we're trying to reach: Saddleback Sam and his wife Samantha. Once you know your target, it will determine many of the components of your seeker service: music style, message topics, testimonies, creative arts, and much more."[14]

The themes of a seeker-focused service will differ from a believer-focused service. Calvary Church (Grand Rapids, Mich.) researched its target audience and then developed the themes of the first six seeker services to answer the following questions: (1) Why is the church full of hypocrites? (2) Would Jesus be a TV evangelist? (3) Is God a Democrat? (4) Is religion for wimps? (5) Would Jesus wear a Rolex? (6) Sex?

The benefit, of course, in offering a seeker-focused service separate from a believer-focused service is that you cover both spiritual conditions that motivate people to attend a church: searching and growing.

You will find that if you offer both a seeker service and a believer service, more believers will attend your seeker service than seekers will attend your believer service. It often surprises church staff to see the large number of members who apparently find spiritual nourishment from the seeker service. This may be because the seeker service is intentionally designed to bring a relevant Christian perspective to issues that "worldly" people are facing. In reality, church members are facing many of these same issues. One of the great benefits of beginning a seeker service, consequently, can be to make the believer service more relevant.

Seeker Hostile

There is such a thing as a "seeker-hostile service." This is a service in which the ritual, liturgy, and in-house jargon are so foreign to a newcomer that he or she feels entirely ignored. The apostle Paul, in speaking to the Corinthian church about the use of tongues in a worship service, presents a broader principle that applies to every church: "If then I do not grasp the meaning of what someone is saying, I am a foreigner to the speaker, and he is a foreigner to me" (1 Cor. 14:11). Paul goes on: "But in the

103

church I would rather speak five intelligible words to instruct others than ten thousand words in a tongue" (1 Cor. 14:19). Why would Paul be so concerned with communication in a commonly understood language? Because he assumed there would be unbelievers in the midst of Christian worship, and it was important that the Christian services not be an obstacle to understanding the gospel: "If . . . some who do not understand or some unbelievers come in, will they not say that you are out of your mind?" (1 Cor. 14:23).

It would make interesting discussion in your church to examine where your present service is on the seeker-hostile/seeker-friendly scale. As a rule, any unexplained words or actions that the newcomer would not understand move you toward the seeker-hostile end of the scale. This includes such rituals as corporate recitation of the Lord's Prayer, the Gloria Patri, or the Apostles' Creed. It includes singing the doxology by memory. It even includes the congregation standing in the service without warning or explanation.

Seeker hostility will be sensed by newcomers in other areas as well, such as acronyms and abbreviations in the bulletin (WMU, Rite 1, UMW, SS) or few or no direction signs to assist visitors throughout the building.

Seeker hostility is most commonly experienced in the reception visitors receive after the service. While most church members don't intentionally shun visitors, most don't go out of their way to greet them, either. This is unfortunate, because my research indicates that most visitors decide whether a church is friendly during the first ten minutes following the conclusion of the service. Members of a seeker-hostile church will leave the newcomer standing alone in the cold. And most of these "foreigners," as Saint Paul calls them, won't return.

The verses in 1 Corinthians 14 suggest that all services, whether believer targeted or seeker targeted, should be seeker friendly. Unfortunately, not all services are. The Service Evaluation Scale in figure 18 can be helpful in considering your present service(s) as well as your new service. Try pinpointing your present service(s) on the scale. If the goal of the service is the greatest outreach to non-Christians for the largest number of conversions, and the experience is designed with the assumption that attenders know little or nothing about "doing church," the service would fall in the upper right quadrant. If the service focuses on the spiritual growth and development of believers, yet is attractive and understandable to non-Christians, it would fall in the upper left quadrant. There are more than a few services I have attended that would be in the lower left quadrant—an exclusive experience focused on, and meaningful only to, long-term believers. And surprisingly, there are even some misdirected services in the lower right. You will want to design your new service in such a way that it falls into the appropriate quadrant.

Figure 18
Service Evaluation Scale

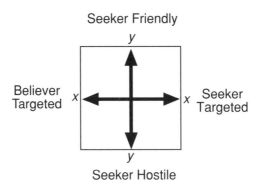

The X axis on this diagram measures the content of the service. The Y axis measures the comfort of the visitor. For example, a service with an emphasis on redemption is seeker targeted. A service with an emphasis on sanctification is believer targeted. If the language is clear and understandable to an outsider, the service is seeker friendly. If the service is filled with religious phrases and jargon, it is seeker hostile.

Your music can also be evaluated on the Service Evaluation Scale. The words of the music (whether seeker targeted or believer targeted) define its place on the X axis. The attractiveness of the music to an unchurched visitor defines its place on the Y axis.

In general, the Y axis evaluates the medium. The X axis evaluates the message.

We have examined the generational group as one variable in defining your new service. The spiritual condition of the target audience is a second variable. There is one final consideration that will help clarify and define your target audience.

Cultural Identity

Approximately half of all Americans consider themselves ethnic.[15] Each year approximately 250,000 people become naturalized American citizens, and thousands more enter the country undocumented. According to the U.S. Center for World Mission, there are 226 distinct people groups in the United States today. And members of these people groups can be found in nearly every town and countryside. Today America is far less a melting pot than it is a stew pot. And sadly, one of the great indictments of the Christian church is that for the most part it has been ineffective in spreading the gospel cross-culturally so Christ is known and worshiped in indigenous cultures and communities. Individuals "tend to resist the outreach efforts of congregations that represent an ethnic, racial, language, socioeconomic, or generational group different from theirs."[16] Until churches—and worship services—are available in a language and location that provide a comfortable ethnic culture for them, there will be many people in America who will never attend church or find faith in God. For some congregations, adding a new service could mean adding a new cross-cultural service.

Not all people, however, have equally strong ethnic identities nor an equal desire to associate with their native culture. As you clarify the target audience for your new service, consider the strength of their ethnic identity. In some cases the answer will be "none." In other cases it will be "much."

The Cultural Identity Scale (fig. 19) is a tool to evaluate whether the ethnic and/or cultural identity of your target audience demands

Figure 19

Cultural Identity Scale

High cultural adaptability	1--2--3--4--5	Low cultural adaptability
Establishment mentality ("I am here to stay")	1--2--3--4--5	Sojourner mentality ("I plan to go home")
Weak native religious identity	1--2--3--4--5	Strong native religious identity
High aspiration to assimilate	1--2--3--4--5	Low aspiration to assimilate
Loss of contact with the community of one's own kind	1--2--3--4--5	Contact with the community of one's own kind
Nonexistence of culturally bounded social organizations (clubs, community centers, associations)	1--2--3--4--5	Existence of culturally bounded social organizations
Nonexistence of culturally bounded mass media (non-English newspapers, radio and television channels)	1--2--3--4--5	Existence of culturally bounded mass media
Lesser social distance (attitude)	1--2--3--4--5	Greater social distance (attitude)
Disappearance of racial discrimination	1--2--3--4--5	Persistence of racial discrimination
Lack of pride in national heritage	1--2--3--4--5	Pride in national heritage
Light skin	1--2--3--4--5	Dark skin
Area with high degree of race mixing	1--2--3--4--5	Area with low degree of race mixing
Exogamous marriages common	1--2--3--4--5	Endogamous marriages common
The second, fourth, or later generation	1--2--3--4--5	The immigrant or the third generation
Frequent change of last name	1--2--3--4--5	Pride in one's name
Upward social mobility	1--2--3--4--5	Minimal upward social mobility
Dispersion of the people in a region	1--2--3--4--5	Concentration of the people in a region
Absence of "power movements"	1--2--3--4--5	Presence of "power movements"
Low consciousness of one's national lineage	1--2--3--4--5	High consciousness of one's national lineage
Residence in a community of under 15% ethnic	1--2--3--4--5	Residence in a community of over 50% ethnic

a new service. Circle one of the five numbers for each trait, based on an analysis of your target audience. If the total score is 75 or above, it is likely that a new service is needed to successfully reach this group.

Determining the ethnic or cultural identity of your new service is important and will require that you select one of the following options.

Identi-Cultural

A new service that is "identi-cultural" will focus on the same piece of the ethnic mosaic as your present service(s) but will differ from your existing service in either generational or spiritual focus. If the score on the above Cultural Identity Scale is below 75 for your target audience, you probably do not need or want a service designed for a different cultural group.

Multicultural

A multicultural service has its identity in diversity. People who are drawn to a multicultural service prefer to worship with people of different cultures. They take genuine pride in the rainbow quality of the service and become uncomfortable when any one cultural group begins to dominate. Rev. Tom Wolf, pastor of The Church on Brady (Los Angeles, Calif.), recounted to me some years ago a conversation he had with an African-American couple following the church's multicultural service. The two came up to him and said, "Brother Tom, I'm afraid we're going to have to leave this church." After a few moments of Tom's probing questions, the husband shared the real reason for their discomfort: "There are too many blacks showing up at the service." At first Rev. Wolf had trouble understanding why a black couple would object to the racial scale tipping toward more African-Americans in the service. Only later did he realize that the homogeneity of that service was its heterogeneity. The departing couple valued— and even thrived on—the diversity of color and culture.

If you are considering adding a multicultural worship service, the generational group most likely to be attracted because of this distinctive will be Baby Boomers. These younger adults tend to be both aware of cultural differences and yet most desirous of crossing traditional cultural boundaries. In contrast, the Senior

108

generation (as a rule) is less inclined to intentionally cross cultural boundaries. Few new services that focus on a senior adult, multicultural target audience are successful. On the other end of the generational spectrum, the Baby Buster generation frequently does not consider cultural differences to be significant enough to attend a service simply because of that distinctive. The Christian Assembly Church (Eagle Rock, Calif.) appears quite multicultural to the first-time visitor (approximately 50 percent Anglo, 35 percent Hispanic, 15 percent Black). But in reality, for the Baby Busters who attend, the cultural plurality is largely irrelevant. The generational focus, on the other hand, is crucial.

Often the third generation of immigrants are attracted to multicultural services. These grandchildren of immigrants frequently feel drawn to their cultural roots but have lived in the Western culture for their entire life and can't or don't want to entirely return to their roots. By contrast, first generation immigrants are more likely to attend a cross-cultural service, and second-generation immigrants are most attracted to identi-cultural services. A multicultural service is usually conducted in only one language—the language of your present service(s).

In addition to Baby Boomers and third generation immigrants, ethnics most likely to attend a multicultural service are those with at least a high school education who interact occupationally with persons of other cultures, then return home to an ethnic community. These "cultural chameleons" are sometimes more comfortable in a service that blends the two cultures in which they live than in a service that excludes either culture.

A multicultural service will reflect its diversity in a variety of ways. The most visible and powerful means of communicating the multicultural nature of the service is in the ethnic diversity of the platform personnel. Choir, worship leader, lay leaders, and musical talent should be an obvious indication that this service is different. The music is the next best means of communicating multiethnicity. Cultural traditions, art, and language should also be intentionally integrated into a new multicultural service.

Remember that a multicultural service will not appeal to most of the people within a particular ethnic group. Indeed, it will appeal to only a small minority within any one cultural group. But with such a service you have the advantage of appealing to several cultural groups and attracting people within those groups who find commonalty in diversity.

Cross-Cultural

If your target audience scores higher than 75 on the Cultural Identity Scale, your new service will need to be cross-cultural in nature. Donald McGavran found that when missionaries want to reach a people group across one or more cultural barriers, the most likely strategy for success is to begin an indigenous church or service. "People prefer to become Christians without crossing barriers," observed McGavran after years of study on the mission field.[17] In reality, when you begin a new service, you are engaged in cross-cultural missions work.

The people most commonly targeted by cross-cultural services are first generation immigrants. The Mountain West Church of God (Stone Mountain, Ga.) has begun three cross-cultural services, one for Russian immigrants, a second for Koreans, another for French-speaking Africans. The Orange Korean Christian Reformed Church (Fullerton, Calif.) began a Spanish-speaking cross-cultural service for those of Hispanic origin in the neighborhood. Christ Lutheran Church (Monterey Park, Calif.), reaches its three primary constituencies by offering an 8:30 A.M. English service, a 10:00 A.M. youth service, and an 11:00 A.M. Chinese service. Cross-cultural services reach individuals and families who would never attend a church service spoken in the mother tongue of the church.

Culture is defined as "a complex of typical behavior or standardized social characteristics peculiar to a specific group, occupation, gender, age, grade, or social class." But while *cultural* is most often used as a description of one's ethnic heritage, it need not be limited to ethnicity. Culture can be defined socioeconomically. Southern Baptists, for example, now have a church in every sizable community in the state of Texas. But visionary leaders are now structuring their church planting strategy to focus on different socioeconomic levels within a given community. They know that the chances of reaching people are greater if they are not asked to cross socioeconomic barriers to come to Christ. The same principle holds for a church considering a new service. A cross-cultural service targeting a specific socioeconomic level is a realistic strategy to reach a new group of people.

Culture can also be defined *geographically*. Joel Garreau suggests that within the borders of North America there are nine distinct geographical cultures that influence people's lifestyles and personal preferences.[18] People displaced from one of these cultures to another often feel like foreigners. If there are sufficient numbers of such "foreigners" in your community, they are a realistic target audience for a new style service. Any true southerner, for example, knows the strong bond that a common southern culture forges between people. There is a Southern Baptist church in Chicago that offers a service for displaced southerners and afterward serves grits and gravy, black-eyed peas, corn bread, and catfish. The culture of the West appeals to some people. Ascension Lutheran Church (Thousand Oaks, Calif.) averages seventy-five to one hundred people at its Saturday night country-western service. At Community Lutheran Church (Las Vegas, Nev.), the Honky-Tonk Angels lead over two hundred people through a similar country-style service.

Still another paradigm of culture, as you consider adding a cross-cultural service in your church, is *liturgical*. Some people (such as those with Roman Catholic backgrounds) have grown up accustomed to a particular liturgical experience in church. And even though they may have long ago departed from active church involvement, they are comfortable with a particular liturgical style. The First Baptist Church (New Orleans, La.) began a cross-cultural service for Jews who were interested in learning more about Jesus but not interested in disowning their Jewish tradition of worship.

Culture can be defined *maritally*. The Orlando Christian Assembly (Orlando, Fla.) has a Saturday night service geared specifically for single men and women. Central United Protestant Church (Richland, Wash.) has a service for families with young children.

111

Figure 20

Selecting Your Target Audience

Generational	Senior	Baby Boomer	Baby Buster
Spiritual	Believer Focused		Seeker Focused
Cultural	Identi-Cultural	Multicultural	Cross-Cultural

In some cases culture can be defined by *lifestyle* or even by *occupation*. The key insight about a cross-cultural service is identified by Sally Morgenthaller: "Whether we're in an urban African-American, border town Hispanic, middle class Caucasian, or rural German environment, we can witness more effectively through worship if we first of all affirm the culture by using its unique 'language,' and, secondly, transcend it with the gospel. It is enculturating the truth into the vernacular of a broken world."[19]

It is not uncommon for some well-meaning people to object that a cross-cultural service smacks of racism and segregation. Others contend that since we are "one in Christ," cross-cultural services create barriers rather than remove them. Personally, I find it a stretch to imagine that I could experience a meaningful encounter with the risen Christ in a service in which the language used was a dialect of Swahili. Yet for those whose culture is a significant source of their identity, that is exactly what we are asking them to do—understand the message of Christ when they cannot even understand the messenger.

Decide What Kind of Service You Want

Based on the three variables—generational group, spiritual condition, and cultural identity—there are theoretically eighteen kinds of services your church could offer! What an exciting choice. But how do you make it? And where do you begin? First, realize that by simply making a choice to add a new service, you are likely on your way to new energy and growth. "The principle of adding a worship service to attract new people *works*," says Don Brandt, "regardless of the style of the new service."[20]

Begin by looking at the three variables together in figure 20.

Here are some guidelines for selecting a target audience for your new service:

First, locate your present service on each of the three variables: generational, spiritual, and cultural. To do this, identify the predominant group in your service and/or the group from which most new members are coming.

Then, to identify a target audience for your new service, move one of the groups in one of the variables.

For example, suppose your present service appeals to Seniors (born before 1946), is believer focused (those professing Christian faith), and is identi-cultural (group shares a common cultural affinity). Visually your service would look like figure 21.

Figure 21

Selecting Your Target Audience

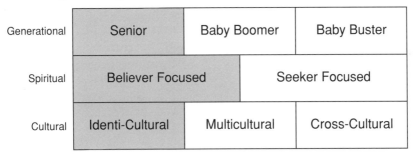

Generational	Senior	Baby Boomer	Baby Buster
Spiritual	Believer Focused		Seeker Focused
Cultural	Identi-Cultural	Multicultural	Cross-Cultural

For your new service to have the best chance of success, change only one of the variables. For example, if you believe that your church's best ministry is to Seniors but you already have one Senior-oriented service, your new service could change the spiritual variable and be a Senior seeker service.

Or if you live in an area where the cultural context is changing, you may decide to retain the Senior and believer focused variables but start a new multicultural service.

One change in one variable will be a significant enough change to attract an entirely new group of people. Changing more than one variable will make the process of researching and planning the new service not just twice as complicated but four times so. Changing all three variables to define your next new service will require a Herculean effort and reduce the chances of success dramatically.

Here's another suggestion based on my research. If you decide to change either the generational or the cultural variable for your new service, limit your move to the adjacent group from where your present service is located. Don't jump over a group. For example, move from Senior to Baby Boomer, not from Senior to Baby Buster; or from identi-cultural to multicultural, not from identi-cultural to cross-cultural. Jumping over a group will make the task of planning and incorporating a new style service into your present ministry considerably more challenging because of the dramatic difference between the new group and your present membership. If you are a Senior church and you desire to reach the Baby Buster generation, start a Baby Boomer service first. Then make your third service for Baby Busters. The same principle applies to the cultural variable.

So if your present service is believer focused, identi-cultural, and appeals to Seniors (fig. 21), you have three new-service options, illustrated by figures 22–24 on the following pages.

Realize You Won't Reach Everyone

The process of selecting a target audience for a new service can be a stretch for some well-intentioned believers. It implies—correctly— that you will not reach everyone in your community. In the video *A Church for the Twenty-First Century,* Leith Anderson comments, "One of the most difficult decisions is to decide who we're *not* going to reach. If there are 50 different groups of people within our area, who are the three or five or seven that we're going to be most effec-

Figure 22

Selecting Your Target Audience

New Service Option 1

Generational: Baby Boomer (born between 1946–64)

Spiritual: Believer Focused (professing Christians)

Cultural: Identi-Cultural (similar cultural identity)

Generational	Senior	Baby Boomer	Baby Buster
Spiritual	Believer Focused		Seeker Focused
Cultural	Identi-Cultural	Multicultural	Cross-Cultural

Figure 23

Selecting Your Target Audience

New Service Option 2

Generational: Senior (born prior to 1946)

Spiritual: Seeker Focused (those persons considering Christianity)

Cultural: Identi-Cultural (similar cultural identity)

Generational	Senior	Baby Boomer	Baby Buster
Spiritual	Believer Focused		Seeker Focused
Cultural	Identi-Cultural	Multicultural	Cross-Cultural

115

Figure 24

Selecting Your Target Audience

New Service Option 3

Generational: Senior (born prior to 1946)

    Spiritual: Believer Focused (professing Christians)

      Cultural: Multicultural (a variety of cultural backgrounds)

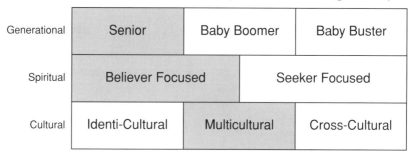

Generational	Senior	Baby Boomer	Baby Buster
Spiritual	Believer Focused	Seeker Focused	
Cultural	Identi-Cultural	Multicultural	Cross-Cultural

tive with? Not that we exclude anyone, but that we target in on those that are most likely to respond to our particular congregation."[21]

Jesus himself tells us to be good stewards of the gospel with the limited resources we have been given, focusing on those people who want to hear and will respond. In Matthew 10:14 he instructs his followers to "shake the dust off your feet" in those towns that would not accept them, and go to those places that wanted to hear. The parable of the sower (Matthew 13) tells us that the gospel will be received in various ways by various people, the implication being that we are to sow in good soil. In Mark 4:9 Jesus says, "He who has ears to hear, let him hear." Christ later tells his disciples to turn their eyes to the fields that are ripe to harvest (John 4:35).

Defining your target group is simply good stewardship. It is investing the resources we have been given, so that upon the return of our Master we can show a return on those resources. In the next chapter we will explore how to begin harvesting.

116

What Kind of Service
Do *They* Want?

∽

Once you have decided on an appropriate target audience for your service, the next step is to design an appropriate service for your target audience. The secret to success is a clear understanding of the people you are trying to reach. What are the important issues in their lives? What are their attitudes about faith, church, God? What are their problems and dreams to which the gospel can speak? Finding the answers to these questions requires research.

"Oh no," you may be thinking. "I believe I'll just skip over this chapter."

Please don't. Inadequate research on your target audience will come back to bite you in declining attendance, declining morale, and declining momentum in the first critical months when you need just the opposite.

If your new service fails for whatever reason (including inadequate understanding of your target audience), you won't be able to generate enough support to try again for three to five years. Do it right the first time. You'll be glad you did.

Remember whom the service is for. It is important to clearly define your target audience because, as Donald Brandt observes, "when additional worship opportunities are created with no particular constituency in mind, the service that results usually reflects the cultural tastes of the present membership, and might not serve

117

constituencies other than the ones already existing in your congregation."[1] Regardless of the kind of new service you are planning, always keep in mind that your target audience is *not* presently active in your church. While some people will move over from your existing service(s), the primary focus of the new service should be: (1) unchurched people in your community, and (2) inactive members in your church and other churches in the community.

The Goal and Value of Research

The research on your target audience has one simple objective: to create a one- to two-page report that succinctly describes the attitudes, needs, interests, concerns, and priorities of your target audience. This document will receive wide circulation in the church and be used to:

- keep leaders informed and supportive of the new service;
- keep the congregation informed and supportive of the new service;
- help the worship planning team design services that are appropriate and relevant;
- evaluate the new service to determine whether it is accomplishing its goals.

The content of a research summary report is discussed in more detail later in this chapter.

Don't assume you know your target audience so well that you need not talk to them. I guarantee that when you explore beneath the surface, you will discover astonishing insights about their world, their priorities, and how the gospel will be meaningful to them.

The research process also provides one of your best opportunities to "convert" church members who may still be reluctant to endorse a new service. Members who become involved in researching your target audience:

- enhance their knowledge of, and desire to reach, the unchurched;
- develop a more personal interest and ownership in the new service;
- find the experience to be one of the more rewarding they have had in the church;
- show others in the church that the project has widespread support;
- enhance their stature as visionary leaders in the church.

Involving members in researching your target audience is an application of an important broader principle: The more who participate in activities related to your new service, the more ownership is created and the more likely it is to succeed.

Research Methodologies

"One of the distinguishing characteristics of effective churches in the twenty-first century is that they place a high priority on reaching unchurched people and frequently invest time and energy in 'asking the customer,'" reports The Leadership Network. "They conduct interviews, focus groups, and surveys that ask unchurched people in their community why they are unchurched."[2]

The most important challenge in your research will be to focus only on people who represent the target audience you've identified by generation group, spiritual condition, and cultural identity (as discussed in chapter 4). Don't research people you're not trying to reach.

Focus Groups

The most helpful research method you can employ is the focus group. This is a research technique first developed by businesses to learn about the needs of their prospective customers. An increasing number of churches are finding that focus groups are an excellent means of learning more about the needs of their prospective members.

Briefly, a focus group is a fifty-minute interview session with a group of eight to twelve people who represent a particular homogeneous group—in this case, your target audience. The focus group is led by a moderator who directs questions and discussion on topics related to your church and your new service. The outcome of your focus groups will be a better understanding of the kind of service that will be relevant and meaningful to this target group. I have included more information on organizing and conducting focus groups in appendix C.

College Church of the Nazarene (Bourbonnais, Ill.) added an interesting twist to the use of a focus group in researching a new service. The church asked focus group members to attend the present service and then share with lay elders (no pastors present) their opinions of the experience. As a result of this input, "the final format was not any of the options the board or staff originally considered."[3] I know of several other churches in which members have asked friends to attend their church for the purpose of evaluating the service from a newcomer's perspective and then asked them to share their thoughts and experiences. It has always provided enlightening insights.

Books and Magazine Articles

You will probably find that some of your research has already been done for you in formulating generalizations about your target audience. Much has been written, for example, on Baby Boomers. Little is available, on the other hand, about people who prefer multicultural services.

If you have members reviewing articles, videos, or books about your target audience, they should compile a one-page summary of each source, identifying the insights related to developing an appropriate new style service.

Telephone Interviews

Professional researchers often conduct one on-one interviews to explore issues with a broader sampling than is possible through focus groups. You can do the same thing. Interviews are best conducted by phone since it is less threatening to the interviewee and makes more effecient use of time for the interviewer. The interview should last no longer than fifteen minutes and can be based on just a few simple questions. For example:

- Are you an active member of a nearby church?
- What do you think is the greatest need of [target audience] in this community?
- Why do you think most [target audience] don't go to church?
- If you were looking for a church in your area, what kind of things would interest you? What would turn you off?
- What advice would you give to churches that wanted to do something for [target audience]?[4]

Surveys

Mailed surveys are not a particularly helpful source of information for generalizing about your target audience or deciding on the components of your new service. Surveys have the potential of misleading your research conclusions by causing you to generalize the characteristics of your target audience from the responses of your survey. In reality they only represent the characteristics of those people who chose to send in the survey. And many times people who choose to send in surveys do not reflect an accurate cross section of a population group. Nevertheless, written surveys can be a useful supplement to other, more reliable sources of information on your target audience. If you decide to use this technique as one source of information, collect a minimum of seventy-five surveys. To collect this number of responses you will most likely need to send out five hundred to a thousand surveys.

121

Questions should be written in a way that allows you to quantify the responses. As an example, question 1 is easier to tally than question 2:

Question 1: Prioritize the following five items as to their significance in your life. . . .

Question 2: What are the most important priorities in your life?

Visit Churches

Earlier I suggested visiting other churches to learn more about how to successfully introduce the idea of a new service to your church. If you found any churches that were focusing on a target audience similar to yours, you will find a return visit to their service will be helpful. (Appendix E will give you some guidelines of what to look for in your visit.)

If the church seems to be a model of the kind of service you are considering, make an appointment with the pastor or worship director. Most people will be happy to share the experience and insights they have gained about their target audience. Here are a few questions that could focus your conversation:

- How long have you been conducting your new service?
- What have you learned about your target audience?
- What were your goals in beginning the service?
- How has the new service changed since you began, and with what results?
- What would you do differently if you had it to do over again?

Videos

Some larger churches videotape their services for either broadcast or distribution. If you know of churches that have a service geared toward a target audience similar to yours, ask whether videotapes are available.

The Research Summary Report

The goal of your research is to produce a report which describes what you have learned about your target audience. Here are suggestions for what to include in your report.

First, as specifically as possible, describe your target audience, including generational group, spiritual condition, and cultural identity.

Next, describe common attitudes, opinions, feelings, needs, and concerns of your target audience in the following areas:

1. Religion and church. What involvement or experience does your target audience have with organized religion? Are these people outside a practicing Christian faith but open to reconsidering their religious lifestyle (seekers)? Or are they practitioners of the faith but not participating in a church (believers)? What opinions do they hold about God, Jesus, prayer, eternal life, forgiveness, salvation, organized religion, your church, your denomination?

2. Needs and concerns. Identify and list the five areas of personal need or concern that are most often mentioned by your target audience. Do they worry about their children? Finances? Health? Death? Friends? Occupation?

3. Culture. How important is their cultural identity to them? Are they first, second, or third generation immigrants? In what languages are they fluent? What language do they speak in their homes? How strongly do they desire interaction and contact with people outside their own language and culture? Would the ethnic flavor of a service affect their likelihood of attending?

4. Music preference. Because the musical style of a service is the single most important ingredient in defining a service, it is important to know what kind of music appeals to this group. Does Christian music exist in this same genre?

5. Service time, location, frequency preference. Are there certain days of the week and times of day that would be more or less preferable for a meeting, based on the lifestyle of your target audience? Are the church facilities a factor (asset or obstacle) to their attendance? Is a weekly service the best option? Biweekly? Monthly?

The Mecklenberg Community Church, near Charlotte, North Carolina, employed a national research firm to survey the surrounding unchurched community regarding attitudes toward church. The question was asked: Why don't you go to church? Here is what they learned:[5]

1. *Churches have too many problems (81%).* The reputation of the church among the unchurched (in this community, at least) is that churches are hypocritical, judgmental, and just plain mean. One man in the survey said, "I have enough problems in my life. Why would I go to church and get more?"

2. *There is no value in attending (74%).* The unchurched felt that they could connect with God as easily, if not better, on the golf course as in a worship service. While interested in spiritual things, the unchurched did not feel that church had much to offer their spiritual pilgrimage. This verdict would be similar to McDonald's discovering that people wanted hamburgers but didn't think McDonald's was a place to get one.

3. *I don't have the time (48%).* Time has replaced money as the new currency in contemporary American society. Rather than asking, "How much does this cost?" people are prone to ask, "How long will this take?" Sundays are for many the only day to play.

4. *I'm simply not interested (42%).* A rather large number of people simply had other things that were more important than attending church.

5. *Churches ask for money too much (40%).* Many felt that churches seemed more interested in their wallets than in them as people.

6. and 7. *Church services are usually boring (36%) and irrelevant to the way I live (34%).* The verdict of some of the unchurched was that most services are boring and lifeless, with sermons irrelevant to the real world.

8. *I don't believe in God, or I am unsure that God exists (12%).* Many Christians feel that the unchurched have rejected faith or God. Actually, a large majority of Americans do believe in God. In reality it seems that most are simply rejecting the church.

Profiling Your Target Man and Woman

Leith Anderson summarizes the simple process of target group evangelism: (1) Decide who is to be reached; (2) learn about those people; (3) discover the most effective means of reaching them.[6]

Some churches find it helpful to create a hypothetical personality profile of people who typify their target audience. Such a profile can help personalize the general characteristics you have learned about your target audience into a "real" person. Develop at least two personality profiles (one male and one female). You may wish to create three or four, with each representing a slightly different subset of your target audience. Variations might include specific age (within the range of your target audience), different marital or family status, different religious attitudes, slightly different ethnic identity. This exercise will help members realize that not everyone in your target audience is an exact replica and that within the broad generational, spiritual, and cultural categories there will be some diversity. Several characterizations of your target audience will also help those planning the service to identify appropriate issues and themes.

Rick Warren describes the profile of his church's target audience: "We've named our composite profile 'Saddleback Sam.' Most of our members would have no problem describing Sam. We discuss him in detail in every membership class. Saddleback Sam is the typical unchurched man who lives in our area. His age is late thirties to early forties. He has a college degree and may have an advanced degree. He is married to Saddleback Samantha, and they have two kids, Steve and Sally. Sam likes his job, he likes where he lives, and he thinks he's enjoying life now more than he was five years ago. He likes contemporary music. He's either a professional, a manager, or a successful entrepreneur. Health and

125

fitness are high priorities for Sam and his family. Sam prefers casual, informal meetings over anything stiff and formal. He is overextended in time and money. He is very materialistic and yet will honestly admit that his wealth has not brought him lasting happiness. He is skeptical of what he calls 'organized religion.'"

Warren concludes, "Why do we go to all this trouble defining the typical person we're trying to reach? Because the more you understand someone, the easier it is to communicate with him."[7]

Using Your Research Summary Effectively

Your research summary report and personality profiles will be an ally for you in many times and places. Once your research group feels that these documents present an accurate description of your target audience, they should be presented to your church leadership. Those who were involved in the research are the best ones to present the material. The research summary should be mailed to board members with a cover letter asking that they review the material prior to the meeting. This letter is a good chance (always be looking for such opportunities) to reaffirm pastoral support and enthusiasm for the new service and the progress the church is making in this exciting new endeavor.

The presentation to the board should be well prepared. This is not just a truism. Church leaders are far more likely to publicly identify with the new service initiative if they have confidence in those who are managing the process. A haphazard presentation with uncertain answers will result in leaders feeling increasingly tentative about the idea, and withholding public support.

During the meeting explain that the step just completed was to learn as much as possible about the target group in order to most effectively reach out to them through the new service. The next step is for the worship planning group to begin translating this research into a service design that retains your nonnegotiables of faith and theology, while presenting the gospel in a meaningful and attractive way to your target group. Let church leaders know that they will be kept informed of progress related to the new service in subsequent meetings.

At the conclusion of the presentation explain that a presentation will be made in a coming Sunday worship service to share the research results with the congregation. The pastor or chairperson should recommend that a statement of continued support for the service and target audience be adopted by the leadership board.

Sharing Your Research with the Congregation

The next important step is presenting your research to the congregation. It is obviously important to be well prepared. Send a copy of the research summary report to members prior to the presentation in the service. Include a cover letter explaining that there will be a special report in the coming Sunday service.

Select a spokesperson who is known and respected in the church and who is a strong proponent of the new service strategy. The pastor should introduce this person and use the opportunity to express appreciation for those members who have been involved in the research process. Naming these people publicly will also position the new service as a project that involves a wide variety of members in the church. The congregation should also be affirmed for their pursuit of Christ's call to make disciples, and be reminded that the new service is a positive response to that call.

A brief biblical lesson can help give the new service a historical perspective in the Christian movement. Just as the early Jewish Christians realized that reaching the Gentiles required a new approach to crossing cultural barriers, so your church is developing new approaches to crossing barriers to reach new people. As Paul said, "I have become all things to all [people] so that by all possible means I might save some" (1 Cor. 9:22). We are called to do the same.

Once the church leaders and members have been brought up to speed on the research of your target audience, the "real world" issues of when to meet and where to hold your new service begin to become important issues. In the next chapter we will help discover the best options for you.

When and Where
to Meet

What is the best day for your new service? What month of the year should it begin? Where is the best location to have it for maximum attendance? What time should it start?

Finding the answers to these questions is important, not because the right answer will cause your service to succeed, but because the wrong answer may well cause it to fail. "Many attempts to add an additional service fail simply due to wrong timing," says Gary McIntosh, editor of *The Church Growth Network*.[1] With all the work that has gone and will go into your new service, you don't want a bad decision here to derail the process.

There are several rules that apply to these questions. We'll look at the rules, then the exceptions.

Rule 1: The best day for your new service is Sunday.

Seventh-day Adventists would beg to differ, and the growth of this denomination is a strong testimony to the fact that services on days other than Sunday can be successful. However, even hardcore atheists know that Sunday is when people go to church.

Exceptions to rule 1:

1. A service that will be so radically different from your present service that it would be considered offensive to many members who come in contact with it on Sunday morning.

This is one reason that some seeker-targeted services will do better on Saturday night.

2. A service geared toward Baby Busters. Two of the best times for this group seem to be Thursday evening at 7:30 P.M. and either Friday or Saturday night at 11:30 P.M.

3. A service for people who work on Sunday. The best alternative is early Saturday evening; the next best is Monday night.

4. A service in the summer for those who take weekend vacations. The best time for this target audience is Thursday evening at 6:30 P.M.

5. A service for Jewish families or individuals. Best day: the Sabbath.

If you are in a church with three successful Sunday services and are considering a fourth on Saturday night because no other time is available, I encourage you to first look for an alternative site to conduct an additional Sunday service. As we will see later, Saturday night services are a considerable challenge. *When* a service is held is far more important to its success than *where* it is held.

Rule 2: The best time to start your new service is 9:00 A.M.

That's good news and bad news. The good news is that you probably already have a service at that time. The bad news is that you probably already have a service at that time.

Exceptions to rule 2:

1. A service for farmers during harvest season. Best time: 7:00 A.M. or before. Best duration: thirty to forty-five minutes. No dress code.

2. A service for those working graveyard shifts on the weekend. Best time: 11:00 P.M. Saturday night. You'll also be surprised at the number of young people who show up at this service. (They love to respond to parental inquiries when they arrive home after midnight, "But Mom, I was at church!")

Rule 3: There is not a rule for the best location of your new service.

Actually, there *are* some important rules for determining the best location of your new service, but they depend largely on the generational group of your target audience. Put simply, one location will not be appropriate for all new services. We'll examine this issue in detail later in the chapter.

When to Meet

The time of your present service(s) and proposed new service may vary somewhat from the times discussed below. But the following observations should be helpful as you consider the best choice for adding a new service to your present weekend options.

From One Service to Two

The schedule most common in churches with one service looks something like this:

Sunday school   9:45 A.M.–10:45 A.M.
Worship service 11:00 A.M.–12:00 P.M.

Scheduling a second service is most successfully handled through one of the following options. These options are not listed in order of preference, since there is no one preferable choice.

Option 1

Service 1	8:30 A.M.–9:30 A.M.
Sunday school	9:45 A.M.–10:45 A.M.
Service 2	11:00 A.M.–12:00 P.M.

For a church with a traditional Sunday school hour followed by morning worship, this schedule option provides the easiest transition to an additional service.[2] The obvious advantage of this option is that it allows for people to attend the educational classes and select the service of their choice, either before or after their class. The closer your educational hour is to your service, the more likely people will stay for both. A second significant benefit is that it allows you to add a new service without disrupting your present schedule.

131

A pastor friend recently told me his church's adult Sunday school attendance grew after the church moved the service ahead of the educational hour. People came to church and stayed for Sunday school. Prior to that only the faithful few came early to attend Sunday school. This highlights an important principle: People are more likely to stay later than come earlier. Consequently, in this scheduling option you will likely have a higher percentage of your first service attending Sunday school than your second.

There is not a common pattern in churches with two services as to which is better attended. Lyle Schaller has observed that the farther east one moves across the country, the more likely the later service will be larger. Conversely, the farther west, the more likely the earlier service will be larger.[3] This pattern seems to extend even to Hawaii, where it is not uncommon to see the 8:00 A.M. service as the most widely attended.

The fact is, however, that if you go from one service to two, you will probably find that attendance at one of them will be at least twice the attendance of the other.[4] Some church leaders wonder whether an early service will be too early for a young adult crowd. It won't be. If you'd like to verify the fact that Baby Boomers are up early on Sunday morning, go visit some of the local restaurants and take an informal age count. You'll find mostly people between twenty-five and fifty years old. Schaller observes that "today's generation of people in the thirty-five to fifty-four age bracket get up earlier in the morning than was true of the same age group in the 1930s. One obvious implication is an earlier hour of worship will be more attractive today than it was in the 1930s."[5] The one exception to this rule may be parents with young children. Services and classes that begin earlier than 9:00 A.M. will not be successful in reaching large numbers of people in this age group.

Option 2

Service 1   9:00 A.M.–10:00 A.M. (location A)
Service 2   9:15 A.M.–10:15 A.M. (location B)
Sunday school   10:30 A.M.–11:30 A.M.

Since 9:00 A.M. Sunday morning is generally a good time to begin a service, this model does not limit you to offering only one service at that time. Simply schedule two services with slightly staggered starting times. College Avenue Baptist Church (San Diego, Calif.) has Sunday morning services at 10:10 A.M. and 10:30 A.M. The 10:10 A.M. service is geared toward Baby Boomer believers and held in the fellowship hall, while the 10:30 A.M. service is designed for older adult believers and held in the sanctuary. The senior pastor preaches at both services.

One benefit of this option is that a family can attend church at the same time. Those who prefer one style of service can go to the sanctuary, those who enjoy a different style can attend in the fellowship hall. The music in both services, while different in style, should focus on a similar theme. Lay testimonies may be shared in both services. The sermon is the same in both services, so participants leave either hour having heard the same message.

Option 3

Service 1	9:00 A.M.–10:00 A.M.
Service 2	10:30 A.M.–11:30 A.M.
Sunday school	6:00 P.M.–7:00 P.M.

In general, a service scheduled before 9:00 A.M. tends to be too early for many. And starting a service that concludes after 12:00 is too late. One strength of this scheduling option is that both services are offered at good times on Sunday morning. Another strength is that it forces the educational hour to be strong enough to stand on its own. For instance, the Fellowship Missionary Church (Ft. Wayne, Ind.) found that moving its Sunday school to Sunday evening gave the church the flexibility to be more creative with its educational focus. Moving the educational hour to Sunday night also frees up Sunday morning to add a third service later.

Option 4

Service 1	9:00 A.M.–10:00 A.M.
Sunday school	9:00 A.M.–10:00 A.M.

133

Service 2   10:30 A.M.–11:30 A.M.
Sunday school   10:30 A.M.–11:30 A.M.

If you have a strong Sunday school program and a variety of classes, one of the best options is to add a new service and a new Sunday school hour simultaneously. Not all classes and age groups need to meet at both hours. When the First Nazarene Church (Pasadena, Calif.) added a second service, adult classes decided when they wanted to meet and which service they wanted to attend. Those in the minority became the nucleus for a new class at the opposite hour.

If you presently have two services and one Sunday school, it is quite likely that an additional Sunday school hour will increase your worship attendance, even without adding a new service. The First United Methodist Church (Osterville, Mass.) found that a second Sunday school hour—begun eight years after their second service was started—significantly increased the number attending the second service.[6] The reason is that, as Southern Baptist Sunday school authority Arthur Flake observed years ago, "new units equal new growth." When you begin new classes, you will attract new people, many of whom stay for the service. Of course, children's activities (nursery through high school) should be available at both hours to accommodate parents' preference in service style.

As you contemplate the best time to begin your new service, another suggestion is to begin the service on the hour or half hour (10:00 A.M., 9:30 A.M.) rather than the quarter hour (9:45 A.M., 10:15 A.M.). Advent Presbyterian Church (Memphis, Tenn.) moved its first service from 9:15 A.M. to 9:30 A.M. and experienced an attendance jump of 20 percent. Pastor David Schieber reported that nothing else changed that would have caused the increase except the starting time.[7]

From Two Services to Three

Most churches that presently offer two services have a schedule something like this:

134

Service 1   8:30 A.M.–9:30 A.M.
Sunday school   9:45 A.M.–10:45 A.M.
Service 2   11:00 A.M.–12:00 P.M.

Scheduling a third service in such churches is best accomplished in one of the following formats.

Option 1

Service 1   8:30 A.M.–9:30 A.M.
Service 2   9:45 A.M.–10:45 A.M.
Sunday school   9:45 A.M.–10:45 A.M.
Service 3   11:00 A.M.–12:00 P.M.
Sunday school   11:00 A.M.–12:00 P.M.

This option has the benefit of leaving your two existing services alone and simply adding the new service in between. If adding a third service requires a significant change in the starting hours of your present service(s), a much greater "sales" effort will be necessary for your present members to buy into the change. You can generally get people to change their worship starting time by a half hour in either direction. But if you plan to ask for more than thirty minutes, spend a good deal of time preparing them for the change.

If you are planning three services with two different styles (that is, two services of one style and one of a second style), the service with a different style should be in the second or third hour, preferably the second.

Many churches offer a service at 9:45 and 11:00. Adding a third service at 8:30 A.M. may be your only option, but it places two burdens on your new service—it will tend to start small because it is new, and it will tend to remain small because it is early. (The exception is Hawaii.)

Option 2

Service 1   6:00 P.M.–7:00 P.M.
                      (Sat., Sun., Mon., Thur., Fri.)

135

Sunday school	7:15 P.M.–8:15 P.M.
	(Sat., Sun., Mon., Thur., Fri.)
Service 2	8:30 A.M.–9:30 A.M. (Sun.)
Sunday school	9:45 A.M.–10:45 A.M. (Sun.)
Service 3	11:00 A.M.–12:00 P.M. (Sun.)

This schedule provides the least amount of interruption to the present schedule of most churches already conducting two services. According to best estimates, more than four thousand churches in the United States offer a Saturday night service of some kind,[8] out of some three hundred thousand Protestant churches in the United States. Most churches find that their Saturday night service is attended primarily by young married adults and singles.[9]

The downside of a non-Sunday service is that the failure rate for such services is high. Paul Mundey found that no more than 20 percent of these services survive for more than a year.[10] A non-Sunday service without supporting education classes will also hurt your total Sunday school attendance and will add to the perception of some that this service is not "real" church. Of course, if you expect that those in attendance don't or won't attend a class, you have no problem. Just be sure that no more than a few of your regular members show up.

Village Baptist Church (Portland, Oreg.) began a Saturday night service after filling its three Sunday morning services. But despite the fact that this growing church had successfully added two new services on Sunday morning, the Saturday night service died for lack of a crowd. Following a "postmortem," the church began its Saturday service again, but this time with a full complement of education classes for children and adults. The new strategy worked and the service took off.

If you are not able to complement your evening service with considerable education support, the best style of service to add is a seeker-targeted service in which attenders are not expected to participate in another church activity.

The days of the week listed in parentheses above reflect the sequence of most desirable to least desirable days for an evening service. This sequence is based on my study of the success rates of churches starting evening services. Sunday night is a close second choice for a new service, behind Saturday. Eastside Christian Church (Seattle, Wash.) conducts six services on a weekend. Pastor Doug Murren says, "Sunday night is a great time to add another service identical to Sunday morning."[11] If you offer different-style services on Sunday morning, the Sunday night service should be identical to your most popular morning service.

In general, evening services and services at a nontraditional hour should be contemporary and less formal. Christ United Methodist Church (Salisbury, Md.) offers a Saturday evening service called Saturday Night Lite that lasts only forty-five minutes. The sign on the outside of the church reads, "Jeans and sneakers expected. No halos required."

Option 3

Service 1	6:00 P.M.–7:00 P.M.
	(Sat., Sun., Mon., Thur., Fri.)
Sunday school	7:15 P.M.–8:15 P.M.
	(Sat., Sun., Mon., Thur., Fri.)
Service 2	9:30 A.M.–10:30 A.M.
Sunday school	9:30 A.M.–10:30 A.M.
Service 3	11:00 A.M.–12:00 P.M.
Sunday school	11:00 A.M.–12:00 P.M.

The difference between this schedule option and the previous one is not so much the service schedule but the Sunday school. For some churches, the idea of three worship services is easy compared with the prospect of three Sunday school sessions. You will need to decide the priority that the traditional Sunday school teaching hour has for your church. You may decide to offer Sunday school at only one or two of the hours. You will find, however, that the fewer Sunday school hours you offer, the lower the overall Sunday school attendance. The principle that growing churches offer choices is true, not just for worship but for Sunday school as well. Adding new classes will positively affect total Sunday school attendance, just as adding a new service will positively affect total worship attendance. Certainly it is more challenging to find teachers and volunteers for the additional classes. But the effort will result in higher attendance in both worship services and Sunday school classes. (For a more comprehensive discussion on church growth principles applied to Sunday school, see *Growth: A New Vision for the Sunday School* by Charles Arn.)[12]

Option 4

Service 1	8:30 A.M.–9:25 A.M.
Service 2	9:45 A.M.–10:40 A.M.
Service 3	11:00 A.M.–11:55 A.M.
Sunday school	8:30 A.M.–12:00 P.M.

One of the more creative approaches I have seen to handling children during a three-service Sunday morning schedule is at Faith Community Church (Covina, Calif.). Rather than conducting three separate Sunday school hours, the church developed Honey Creek University. It is a continuous flow of activities for three and a half hours on Sunday morning. Learning segments at Honey Creek are twenty minutes each and include activities such as Amazing Discoveries (a science teacher illustrating scriptural truths through demonstrations and learning experiments), the Honey Creek Band (children participating with their own variety of instruments), Acts Alive (dramatic vignettes of Bible stories portrayed in modern settings with children watching and participating), Power Breaks (a half hour of games and activities teaching cooperation and teamwork), and a Bible Discovery session (teachers creatively presenting one insight from Scripture). Honey Creek University has its own mascot—an eight-foot lion (the church treasurer can often be found inside). Students receive "honey dollars," which are earned for positive involvement and good behavior and may be used to purchase items at the Honey Creek store. Because the "university" activities are divided into short, independent segments, children can easily come and go throughout the morning.[13]

Beyond Three Services

Churches that already offer three services often decide that the next logical step is a new sanctuary to allow the entire church to worship together. That is one option. But I do not believe it is the best option. In fact, it may be the worst. There is much risk, with not much gained, in building a sanctuary to accommodate all worshipers at one time and place. Not only will you find a large contingent of unhappy people who feel they have lost "their" service, but the building process itself has proven to be a wolf in sheep's clothing for many churches. A recent issue of *The Win Arn Growth Report* highlighted four reasons why most churches should think twice before building:[14]

1. *The problem of psychological displacement.* With every new building program comes an inevitable displacement of the congregation. The result is a collective disorientation of the church body. The uneasiness of this displacement can nurture an atmosphere of tension, depression, and hostility.
2. *The problem of anticipation letdown.* The average church building program lasts three years. During that time the congregation and pastor idealize the new building as a panacea for all ills, assuming that the church's problems are all building related.
3. *The problem of program lag.* Suddenly the building is finished. Program planning seldom keeps pace with building planning, and the old activities seem obsolete and inadequate in the new structure.
4. *The problem of transitional grief.* Members become attached to church buildings. Though the structure may be archaic, those who feel the body is "abandoning the church" will experience grief and often guilt. As irrational as it may seem, new members and the pastor are likely targets of the resulting anger.

Ray Bowman has written an excellent book titled *When Not to Build*, in which he suggests a number of compelling reasons why a building program can do more harm than good to a growing church.[15] One study found that there are more pastoral breakdowns (physical, mental, moral) within one year of a church building program than at any other time in a pastor's career.[16]

The truth is, however, that if your church already conducts three services on a weekend, your options are limited in adding new services on Sunday morning. Since the principle of new services equal new growth does not end once you arrive at three services, the question is: Where do you go from here?

Simultaneous Services

A growing number of innovative churches are offering two services at the same time. Eastside Christian Church (Fullerton, Calif.) conducts two services (9:00 A.M. and 10:35 A.M.) geared toward older Baby Boomers and younger Seniors in the sanctuary. Two other services, going on simultaneously in the fellowship hall, are geared toward Baby Busters.

In the summertime, Prince of Peace (Burnsville, Minn.) offers an indoor traditional service in the sanctuary at the same time as an outdoor contemporary service on the front lawn.

Actually, modern movie theaters have been practicing the concept for years. Drive by the nearest mall and try to find a theater with less than four movies showing simultaneously. More choices equal more customers. Granted, it's easier to turn on a movie projector than to present a live service every week. But multiple and concurrent use of your facilities can give you more options for more services.

Here's a mind-stretching idea for an entrepreneur of tomorrow. Imagine sometime in the future driving to a downlink church site. Inside are five to ten different worship centers similar to a multiscreen movie theater complex. Each center is receiving a different broadcast from a megachurch somewhere in the country, and people select their preferred service. Would you like a high liturgical mass? Sanctuary 3 has the All Saints Episcopal service. Prefer a country-western service? Choose sanctuary 7 for the Community of Joy service. Are you a Baby Buster? You'll want to try sanctuary 5 for the New Song broadcast. Child care is available for all ages throughout the morning, and education classes are also provided. Well, just a thought.

A Satellite Congregation

A relatively new approach to extending the ministry of the larger church is through a satellite congregation. First introduced by the Southern Baptist denomination, a satellite congregation does not limit services to the existing church campus. A church purchases or rents a facility in a nearby location and conducts one or more additional services at that second location. Services are led by church staff and are scheduled so that the senior pastor can drive to the satellite location to deliver the sermon. (A large church in Atlanta used to fly the pastor by helicopter to its satellite location!)

Colonial Presbyterian Church (Kansas City, Mo.) offers two services in the sanctuary on Sunday morning, along with two concurrent services elsewhere on campus and a fifth service in a Catholic high school several miles away (using the parking lot of the Jewish synagogue next door).

St. Andrew Presbyterian Church (Tucson, Ariz.) purchased a church building across the street from its facility and uses it for a fourth Sunday service staggered over two of its other services.

I know of several churches that are, at this writing, studying a variation of the satellite concept. These churches have television ministries, and their service is broadcast locally on Sunday morning. Their idea is to create one or more "downlink" sites around the city, where the service would be hosted live by a staff member, with certain portions of the service (sermon, announcements, special music) broadcast from the mother church.

At first this sounded a bit impersonal to me. But later I was talking with a member of the Fullerton Evangelical Free Church (Fullerton, Calif.) who told me that their services are often so full that an overflow room is required for those unable to find a seat. In this separate room members view the service on a large-screen monitor. What surprised me was this member's comment that he thinks the seats in the overflow room are better than those in the sanctuary. He told me others also prefer to worship there. It isn't a big jump in conceptual thinking to move from an overflow room to an off-site, downlink congregation.

Midweek Services

A few churches are clear enough about their mission that they are willing to "inconvenience" their members by offering their believers' worship services on Wednesday and Thursday evenings. This frees weekends (prime churchgoing time) for services geared toward unbelievers. Willow Creek Community Church (South Barrington, Ill.) is probably the best-known example of this paradigm, but there are clones following a similar style. Establishing a new church with this schedule is far easier than changing to this schedule later. I do not know of any examples of established churches that have successfully changed their existing Sunday service to an entirely seeker-oriented focus and moved their believers' service to midweek.

Monthly Services

It is far better to conduct one quality new service per month than four mediocre new services per month. In fact, some people who come from an unchurched background will attend a service monthly but not weekly. The Church of the Nazarene (Denver, Colo.) sponsors a monthly Saturday night event with high quality "entertainment" that attracts a considerable number of unchurched people. In fact, the church has placed such a premium on quality that it actually prints tickets for the event. This "service" (no one in the church calls it that) has been the first point of contact for many unchurched people who later began attending other services.

Plant a Church

One of the best ways to participate in Christ's disciple-making mandate is to start a new church. In this approach a nucleus of members is encouraged to leave the mother church and begin a new congregation some miles away. The size of that nucleus depends on the size of the church. Bob Logan suggests that fifty is a minimum number for a first service.[17] Grace Church (Edina,

Minn.) determined it needed two hundred members to begin its new church.

Among researchers and church growth authorities, there is almost universal consensus that planting a new church is the best means of reaching new people with the Good News. And according to an American Baptist study, the majority of mother churches that send out a number of their own members to plant a new church soon regain that number or more.[18]

Scheduling and Change

Here are two things to remember when considering a change in your present schedule to accommodate a new service:

1. The longer you have gone without changing your present schedule, the more difficult will be the change.
2. The more significant the reorganization of your Sunday schedule, the more difficult will be the change.

As a rule, members will more readily accommodate a new service if it does not interrupt their present schedule. Sometimes, however, the service schedule must be modified to allow for growth. The chart in figure 25 identifies the percentage of members likely to accept the scheduling change based on (1) the length of time you have gone without a change in schedule, and (2) the growth pattern of your church during that period of time.

If you must make any changes in your present schedule (even moving the service back or ahead by fifteen minutes), here are two steps that should precede the public announcement of the change:

1. Poll the congregation as to its willingness to slightly alter the worship schedule for the purpose of ministering to additional people in need. My experience with churches that have conducted such congregational surveys is that most members (usually over 80 percent) give a positive response when asked their attitude toward a change in the service schedule if it means reaching and accommodating more people. Plan how best to introduce the idea to get a supportive vote for the freedom to change. This could

Figure 25

Likelihood of Members Accepting a Change
in Sunday Morning Schedule

Years Since the Last Change in Worship Service Schedule	Church's Growth Pattern During This Time Period *	Percent of Members Likely to Support a Schedule Change** with Little or No Resistance
8+ years	growth plateau decline	50% 20% 40%
5–8 years	growth plateau decline	60% 30% 30%
3–5 years	growth plateau decline	70% 40% 20%
0–3 years	growth plateau decline	80% 40% 30%

* growth: (more than + 5% a yr.)
plateau: (+5% to -5% a yr.)
decline: (more than -5% a yr.)

** *Change* is defined as a starting time more than fifteen minutes sooner or later than the previous starting time.

include an initial presentation by the pastor, followed by several respected laypersons sharing their conviction about and enthusiasm for the new service. Don't ask, "Would you support the change in schedule?" Rather, present the recommended schedule and ask, "Would you be able to continue attending the service if it were moved to _____?"

2. *Gain the support of key opinion-makers prior to the announcement of the new schedule.* This should be accomplished in much the same way you solicited support for the new service initiative

144

(see chapter 3). Informal breakfasts or lunches are excellent times for generating support for the schedule change among leaders. Meetings can be one-on-one or with groups of individuals or couples. Explain your ideas and the alternatives regarding schedule changes and solicit their suggestions. Share with leaders the fact that a church's tendency is to resist change and that their support for the new schedule among friends and fellow members will be important for congregational acceptance.

Once you have established the new schedule, stick with it throughout the year. Don't change in the summer. Changing the schedule twice or more a year can have a negative impact on worship attendance.[19] Westminster Presbyterian Church (Duluth, Minn.) had traditionally combined its two different style services into one for the summer. In 1996 the church kept the two-service schedule for the first time throughout the summer. The following September, attendance was up by eighty people over the previous year.

The only exception to this "no summer schedule change" rule is when you add a service.

Where to Meet

The common—yet often ill-conceived—decision of many churches is to conduct all services (including their new one) in the same facility, generally the sanctuary or worship center. It is wise, however, to take a closer look at location alternatives, since this is an important ingredient in the success of a new service.

Before it is possible to determine the best location for your new service, you must consider the target audience for whom the service is designed. Whom the service is for will determine where the service should be.

If your new service is focused on the same generational group as your present congregation but on a different spiritual or cultural segment (see chapter 4), your present sanctuary is probably adequate and appropriate. If your new service is focused on a generational group other than your present constituents, a different room in the church facility—or an entirely different location—may be better.

145

Here is a guide for identifying an appropriate facility, based on the generational group of your target audience. Of course, you can have a successful service in all kinds of facilities. But if all else is equal, try to find the following:

Generational Group	Ideal Facility
Senior	Outside looks like a church building; inside looks like a sanctuary.
Baby Boomer	Outside looks like an office building; inside looks like a theater.
Baby Buster	Outside looks like a storefront; inside looks like a multipurpose room.

On the Church Campus?

The appearance of your present church facility is the most important consideration in determining whether to use it for your new service. Does the architecture give a good first impression? What do people think when they step inside? "Church design has changed dramatically in the last generation," says Ray Bowman, church consultant and architect. "People can tell buildings from the 60s as quickly as they can tell clothes from the same era. Both non-verbally communicate an out-dated message."[20]

Assessing your property's first impression is not always easy, particularly for members who have been attending for over ten years. One good way to do so is to invite someone (representative of your target audience) to visit your church, and then listen to the person's impressions. (Most uninvited visitors will not give you an honest or comprehensive opinion of your facility.) Incidentally, Lyle Schaller suggests that the two critical areas that must give a good first impression are the nursery and the women's restroom.[21]

Another consideration in evaluating your facility is simply whether there is adequate parking. Unless you are taking the new

146

service to your target audience (senior retirement home, city park, skid row mission, Indian reservation) you will need parking. The rule of thumb is one parking stall for every 2.5 people you expect in the service. The well-known 80 percent rule also applies to parking lots; that is, if your parking lot is filled to 80 percent or more for four months, it is unlikely that additional growth will occur.

Still another factor in determining whether your facility is appropriate for the new service is the socioeconomic level of your target audience. Sociologists identify five distinct socioeconomic levels that define most communities: upper, upper-middle, middle, lower-middle, and lower. Dr. Flavil Yeakley found that people at or slightly below the average socioeconomic level of a church's membership will be most comfortable in that facility.[22] If your members' socioeconomic status is middle income, for example, you could expect to use your present facility if the status of your target audience is middle to lower-middle income. If, however, the status of your target audience is upper income, your present facility would not be the best place for the new service.

Next consider the capacity of your sanctuary in comparison with the number of people you expect. An empty room communicates an unspoken message that church is irrelevant. Keep in mind that a room can have different seating capacities. "An empty or full service," says Gary McIntosh, "is based more on the seats available than the actual size of the room. If possible, remove chairs or pews and widen aisles to make the worship service seem fuller."[23]

The following room capacity ranges can be helpful to determine where to meet and how to arrange the seating:[24]

Room Capacity	Unspoken Message	Growth Potential
0–30%	uncomfortably empty	unlikely
30–40%	awkwardly empty	low
40–60%	comfortably empty	fair
60–85%	comfortably full	ideal
85–100%	uncomfortably full	low

Off the Church Campus?

A proven approach for starting new churches is to meet for months (often years) in a rented facility. A school, restaurant, or hotel conference room provides flexibility for space needs and offers a neutral meeting site. The same benefits apply to an established church that adds a new service. Site flexibility and site neutrality are your allies. Commenting on the use of nonchurch facilities for a new service, Robert Lee notes, "Since these structures resemble places where unchurched people shop or do business, they feel safe and comfortable."[25]

I know of churches that have successfully begun a new service in bowling alleys, hotels, restaurants, high schools, retirement homes, Elks lodges, community colleges, funeral parlors, dance lounges, office buildings, and even in the fo'c'sle of an aircraft carrier. (The fo'c'sle is the front of the ship where the anchor chain is retracted. The command chaplain aboard the USS *Independence* believed that a new service outside the ship's chapel would attract sailors who might not otherwise attend. Attendance increased 1200 percent.)

An outdoor service will attract walk-ins who would not otherwise attend, particularly in a location where people naturally congregate (a park, campground, parking lot). An up-tempo, attractive service in a strategic outdoor location will expose a significant number of people to your church for the first time. A well-designed brochure can introduce the church to interested people, listing the benefits available. If such a service sounds vaguely familiar, it's because it was successful several generations ago in a slightly different form: a camp meeting. What goes around comes around!

Taking the service to where the people are is certainly not new, by the way. In the eighteenth century, John Wesley and George Whitefield transformed the religious life of North America and England as they took to the streets and fields to bring their message to the unchurched masses. "In effect," says James White, "the English evangelists were reaching a new audience, those who had never darkened the door of a church."[26]

148

Figure 26 is a flowchart that summarizes the key decisions regarding the location of your new service.

Figure 26

Key Decisions Concerning Location

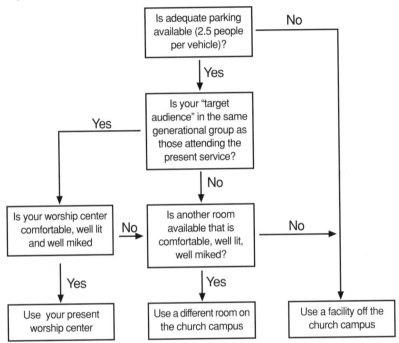

When to Begin the Service

In general, there are good times and not-so-good times during the calendar year to begin a new service. Here are the various options in order of preference:

Good Choices	First preference	September 1–October 30
	Second preference	March 1–April 30

149

	Third preference	November 1– December 31
Poor Choices	Fourth preference	May 1–June 15
	Fifth preference	January 1– February 28*
	Sixth preference	June 16–August 31

* In the Sun Belt states these dates are a fourth preference.

Selecting certain times of year to begin your service builds on what has been called the two-humped-camel phenomenon.[27] Most church attendance figures look something like figure 27.

If you begin your new service on the upswing of a natural high in church attendance, you will benefit from a slingshot effect and start when the best possible attendance can be expected. Then hopefully a sufficient nucleus can be established to carry the new service through the natural lows that will follow. For most churches the best natural upswing comes during the weeks following Labor Day. As a rule, fall is the best time of year to begin a new service. The second-best time is two to four weeks prior to Easter.

In chapter 3 I suggested that the new service be introduced to church leaders and members as an experiment. I have found it takes at least four months (preferably six months) before a valid

Figure 27

Annual Attendance Pattern for Most Churches

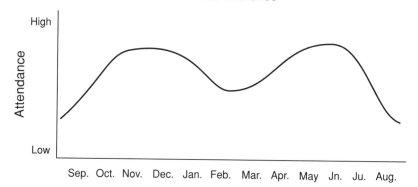

assessment can be made of a new service. However, Elmer Towns suggests three months.[28] Gary McIntosh recommends nine months.[29] Whatever length you decide upon, at the end of the experiment you should conclude one of the following:

- The service meets a need and should be extended indefinitely.
- The service is meeting a need but should be slightly modified and extended indefinitely.
- The service has the potential of meeting a need but should be temporarily discontinued and redesigned, with a new date set to begin again.
- The service doesn't meet a need and should be discontinued.

You have decided when the new service will be held, and where it will be held. The leaders and congregation have been alerted and have consented to the change. Now the fun begins—designing a service that will attract and hold new people.

Designing
the Service

Based on the last four years of my research, there is one factor responsible for more new service failures than anything else: faulty service design. The music, content, style, and themes of most unsuccessful services were inappropriate for their target audience. Sadly, when creative thinking is most needed for the success of the new service, it is often in least abundance.

The purpose of this chapter is to consider issues in designing a successful new service. You may wish to adapt the suggestions to your situation. But please recognize that this step is extremely critical. It is not the only thing involved in a successful new service. But it may well be the most important. Give the service planning and execution the full measure of your dedication and creativity.

Two Foundational Principles

There are two constant, overarching principles to remember as you design your new service. The first principle is: *The sermon is not the message; the service is the message.*

A common assumption in churches is that the sermon is the most important ingredient in the worship. So ingrained is this assumption that the sermon is often referred to as "the message" by members and preacher alike. As a result, Paul Anderson has observed, "pastors may spend fifteen hours on sermon preparation and fifteen minutes throwing the service together."[1]

A better paradigm for the design of your new style service begins with a different assumption: The message is conveyed via the *entire* service.

The goal of your new service is to communicate practical, applicable spiritual truths so participants incorporate these insights into their lives. In reality, this goal may or may not always be accomplished through a twenty-five-minute sermon. That's a hard one to swallow, I know. But if you can reframe your thinking in this way, it will be a wonderful, freeing breakthrough in your new service planning.

The second key principle for designing a successful new service is: *Well-attended services are well-prepared services.*

To a great extent the quality of the service determines the impact of the message. A high-quality service does not guarantee growth, but a low-quality service does guarantee nongrowth. *Quality* describes the music, preaching, drama, pace, transitions, platform personnel, lighting, acoustics, and facilities. The cold, hard reality is that if you want your new service to be successful, you will need to be sure it is high quality.

Think Like an Instructional Technologist

My postgraduate degree is in the field of instructional technology. This is the study of how to facilitate the greatest learning, given (1) the unique characteristics of the learner, (2) the specific objectives, and (3) the variety of instructional media available. The task of an instructional technologist is to create a learning experience that will most likely result in the desired behavior change of the student.

The goal of a worship planner is similar to an instructional technologist: namely, to (1) consider the unique characteristics of those attending the service, (2) identify the specific objectives of the particular service, and (3) determine the mix of communication

154

media that will create a learning experience and behavior change. (Incidentally, instructional technology studies reveal that the unsupported spoken word—which describes the communication style of most sermons—is one of the weakest mediums for changing behavior.)

This instructional technology approach to worship service planning may mean there are some weeks in which no sermon is delivered at all. Some services may have no music. Some sermons may be entirely dramatic presentations. A service designed with the understanding that the entire service is the message will more creatively and dynamically integrate communication media into an optimum learning experience.

Two Ingredients in Every Service

So if the service is the carrier of your message, what is the content of that message? It is my conviction that two themes should be present, regardless of the kind of service you are planning, the target audience you are focusing on, or the theological persuasion from which you come. The themes are:

1. *You are loved*. This is it. Put the Christian faith and its influence in our lives into one simple package—it is love. God's love for us, and our love for God expressed through our love for others (see Matt. 22:37–40).

If the unchurched people who attend your new service can really come to believe that they can be loved—by a personal God and by God's personal family—they have taken a giant step toward establishing their own personal relationship with that God of love. Bob Bast, in the book *Attracting New Members,* correctly observes that "people who come to worship—churched and unchurched alike—already know they are sinners. They don't need to be convinced of that. What they doubt, or cannot believe, is the reality and depth of God's love for them. That note of grace, and unconditional love, needs to be expressed again and again throughout the service. It needs to be ringing in their ears on their drive home."[2]

155

2. There is hope. Love helps us manage the present; hope helps us face the future.

Hope does not deny there will be problems. But hope means those problems can be handled. For the unchurched man or woman on the street, it is a tantalizing idea that there may actually be a way to make sense out of a seemingly senseless life. A service that rings with hope says that change is possible; it says that you can be better; it says that it really may be possible to find meaning in life.

Lyle Schaller observes, "The one theme that is common to churches that are attracting more people is the theme of hope. . . . That note of hope and optimism about the future is a powerful factor in determining the size of the crowd."[3]

Recruit a Worship Planning Team

Consider this rather unsettling paradox: The more services you have planned in your life, the less likely you can successfully plan your new style service.

Most pastors have considerable experience in planning one particular style of service. They are familiar with the sequence. They are comfortable with the ritual. But ask pastors to design a service with a style in which they have little or no experience, and you are asking a great deal—in some cases, the impossible. For most, the new service style is unfamiliar. It is uncomfortable. And it is unlikely that such well-meaning pastors can pull it off single-handedly. If you feel you may fit into this category, a word of caution and a word of advice before you begin:

Caution: Don't depend on your own intuition.
Advice: Involve others in the process.

So how do you make sure that God's love and hope are effectively communicated to the people you are trying to reach? The first important step is the creation of a quality worship planning team.

A worship planning team (WPT) is a group of five to eight creative men and women responsible for designing, planning, and presenting the new service. Churches that have created a new service that is now flourishing almost always have a WPT behind the scenes.

Here are four important benefits of recruiting an effective worship planning team:

1. It will add creativity, variety, and interest to your services.
2. It will utilize the strengths, insights, and gifts of others in the body.
3. It will require you to plan the services farther in advance.
4. It will result in a more polished and professional presentation.

Howard Griffith, pastor of First Christian Church (Shelbyville, Ky.), used his three-month sabbatical to visit the worship services of growing churches. He observes, "At first glance, the worship style of rapidly growing congregations seems informal. Looking closer, it becomes apparent that the worship service is tightly structured and well-scripted."[4] The professional presentation of a service is never by accident. Almost all well-done and growing services have a worship team behind the scenes that is responsible for their success.

Who Is on the Team?

The WPT should be chaired by a worship director. This person (lay or professional) is responsible for the entire worship experience. His or her task is to be sure that all aspects of the service are well planned, rehearsed, and well presented. The role of the worship director is similar to the film director of a motion picture. Film directors do not decide what the movie will be about; that's the producer's (pastor's) job. And film directors do not appear on the screen; that's the job of actors (platform personnel). What film directors do is coordinate production, coach actors, blend ingredients, and orchestrate the entire production into a smooth, coherent, moving experience for the viewers (congregation). The worship director may never appear on the platform, but the ultimate responsibility for a well-presented service largely rests on this individual. My recommendation is that someone other than the pastor serve in this role, even in smaller churches.

A worship director should have good people skills, leadership ability, creativity, and administrative gifts. This individual is so important to the success of a new service that:

1. you should not set a date for your first service until you have identified and trained a worship director;
2. you should immediately begin looking for an apprentice who can work with the worship director to learn the position.

In addition to the worship director, the following individuals should be on the worship planning team:

- pastor
- worship leader (the platform emcee)
- music coordinator
- drama coordinator
- engineer (sound, lights, props)
- two to three people who know the target audience, are creative, and understand the dynamics of effective communication. These people should rotate off the WPT every six months to keep creativity fresh and involvement high.

Consider several people on the WPT from outside your immediate church membership. Pete Ward describes his conclusions after studying the ingredients of an effective Baby Buster, seeker-targeted service: "Real alternative worship will only be created by young people who are culturally and socially outside the church. It will reflect their ways of speaking and relating, and of course their kinds of music. Christian adults cannot provide alternative worship for young people."[5]

If you already have a group that plans your present service, do not use the same people to plan the new service. They will not be

158

able to effectively plan two services with two different styles. And even if they could, the time involved would be too much to ask of anyone other than paid staff.

Just as important as getting the right people on the worship planning team is avoiding the wrong people. Avoid people who have no intention of participating in the new service. Avoid people with a long record of involvement in a service style different from the kind you are planning. And avoid people who are not fully supportive of the commitment to broaden the church's ministry through a new service. Recruit members of the WPT by personal invitation. Do not make a public announcement in the pulpit, bulletin, or church newsletter.

To determine whether you have an adequate team in place, ask yourself the question, Can every element required in the presentation of the new service be accomplished by or delegated to someone on the worship planning team?

What Does the Team Do?

For each service the worship planning team has four objectives:

1. Identify the *theme* of the service. The team should clearly describe the problem or challenge that currently exists in the lives of the target audience, the reason the situation exists, and the symptoms that result from failure to adequately deal with the issue.
2. Identify *attitudes* that attenders bring to the service. What are the viewpoints toward that situation among those in attendance? Why do they feel and act the way they do? What are the obstacles that keep people from solving their problem?
3. Identify the *message* that the service will communicate. What is the solution, and the steps for participants to implement that solution? What are the benefits of paying the cost for change?
4. Identify the best way to *communicate* that message. Participants in the service should be guided through a dynamic

159

interaction of listening, reflecting, questioning, participating, applying, and remembering the experience. How will that best happen?

A Planning Retreat

Your WPT should have two weekend planning retreats per year. The goal of the retreat is to complete the first three steps (above) for a six-month period. That is, the team should leave the retreat with: (1) a list of issues or themes for the next twenty-six weeks, (2) a list of common attitudes and obstacles to solutions, and (3) a simple explanation of the message that participants will leave with after each service. Obviously, the research that was done previously on your target audience will be essential at this point; don't leave home without it!

The Theme Planning Sheet (fig. 28) will help members of your WPT organize their thoughts for each service. The first three items (Theme, Attitudes, Message) should be completed for each service of the next six months by the time you finish the retreat. If suggestions for the fourth step (Ways to communicate the message) grow out of your retreat, they can be noted.

At the end of the retreat give one set of Theme Planning Sheets to each member of the WPT. A loose-leaf notebook is helpful to organize the material. Ask each member to keep this notebook handy and jot down ideas that come to mind in subsequent days for effectively communicating the messages for the next six months. Encourage team members to be constantly on the lookout for illustrations or ideas related to the themes of the services. Real-life stories, cartoons, anecdotes, television shows, news stories, and articles appropriate to the themes can be added to the notebook. This approach will avoid the need for all the creative thinking to occur during the worship planning meeting itself.

What Happens in a Planning Team Meeting?

The goal of your weekly WPT meetings is to focus on the fourth objective—communicating the messages most effectively. The

160

Figure 28

Theme Planning Sheet

Service date:

Theme of the service:

Common attitudes:

Message:

Ways to communicate the message through:

    Music:

    Drama:

    Sermon:

    Testimonies/Interviews:

    Other:

actual planning process should begin approximately six weeks prior to the service. Because you will always have six upcoming services in the works, time should be spent at each meeting on all six. Here is a timeline for service planning and activities:

Six weeks: Review the Theme Planning Sheet for that Sunday with the worship team. Distribute a copy of the Service Planning Sheet (see fig. 29). The first part of this sheet (all the material in the Focus section) should be already completed by the pastor. Spend five minutes reviewing the focus of this service with team members and asking for their ideas.

Each WPT member has the assignment to come to the following week's meeting with the rest of the Service Planning Sheet completed with his or her ideas on special readings, music, drama, testimonies, video, or other media by which the message could be communicated.

Five weeks: Everyone on the WPT shares ideas on the service and how it can be most effective. Group brainstorming is a creative and fun experience.

The assignment of the worship director is to bring a rough draft of this service to the following meeting, including songs, testimonies, and so on. The Order of Service sheet (see fig. 30) is recommended for this purpose, with only the Activity column completed at this point.

At this meeting, the WPT approves publicity planned to promote the service. (See chapter 8.)

Four weeks: The rough draft of the service is finalized. Music is identified and personnel contacted.

Three weeks: All items in the service are finalized and reviewed. The first walk-through of the service is done to evaluate flow, estimate time, and review transitions.

Complete the other columns on the Order of Service sheet. Time should be to the nearest minute, or less if necessary. The Leader column lists who on the platform is responsible for each activity. Use the Notes column to help with the flow and transitions (such things as "Screen goes down," "Sound

162

Figure 29

Service Planning Sheet

Focus

    Title:

    Principle:

    Scripture:

    Key verse:

    Key word:

    Outline:

    Key thoughts:

Verbal

    Testimonies:

    Sharing question:

    Special readings:

    Application project:

Musical/Dramatic

    Music:

    Drama/Sketch:

Visuals

    Multimedia:

    Platform decor:

Other Celebration Ingredients

    Mission moments:

    Moment of response:

    Following the celebration:

Figure 30

Order of Service

Date: _____

Participants meet in _____ at _____

Time	Activity	Leader	Notes	Technical Notes

must start on cue"). The Technical Notes column is for people who are responsible for sound and video.

Two weeks: Modifications to the service plan are made and the second walk-through is completed. Bulletin content is finalized.

One week: All participants meet for prayer and final walkthrough.

One hour before: Preservice prayer is said, last-minute review is made, and questions are answered.

A Worship Leader

The traditional approach to service planning is to determine the activities of the service (special music, announcements, offering, sermon, solo), then designate a person responsible for each activity. During the service, each person performs his or her responsibility, followed by the next person on the schedule, until everyone has accomplished his or her task and the service is over. The result is at best a collection of independent yet related activities. At worst it is a hodgepodge of unrelated and confusing experiences. In any case we hope God has used some part of the service to say something to someone. And we go home.

But the new paradigm demands more. Remember, the service is the message. Making sure this message is clear is the primary task of the worship leader. This person is on the platform to facilitate communication, to orchestrate continuity, and to effectively tie each element into a clear part of the overall message of the service. He or she is the conductor of the symphony.

For some pastors the idea of a worship leader (other than the pastor) is threatening. Even though there may be others who participate in the present service, at least the pastor is center stage during the most important (or at least most lengthy) part of the service—the sermon. But the idea of a person other than the pastor receiving such regular visibility in each and every service may begin to gnaw at a weak ego.

In reality, however, a worship leader actually strengthens the pastor's spiritual leadership in the eyes of the congregation.

Whereas the worship leader's activities leading up to the sermon should clarify the problem, the pastor's role is to clarify the answer.

Obviously, the worship leader must have certain skills and qualifications. He or she should:

- be confident that God has a message to bring to the people;
- understand what that message is;
- be comfortable and communicative in front of an audience;
- be respected by the congregation for modeling a godly example;
- be able to read the moods of an audience.

Some worship leaders are multitalented and, in a more contemporary style service, will sit at a piano or synthesizer, using the microphone to make the transition from one event to another. In more traditional services, worship leaders will sit on the platform and move to the microphone at the appropriate times.

A worship leader will typically open the service with a summary of the issue upon which the service will focus. He or she will verbalize the questions many people have, related to the issue, the problems that result, and the conviction that answers are available as we explore God's Word. Throughout the service it is the responsibility of the worship leader to keep people oriented and on track in that journey from issues to answers.

Ingredients of an Effective Service

Given the fact that the service is the message, what are the tools available to the worship planning team to best communicate that message?

Music

Music is the most important ingredient in a successful service. Good music equals a good service. Poor music equals a poor service. Of course, good music plus good preaching plus good drama plus good pace plus good transitions equals a great service. So don't underestimate the importance of the mix of components that attract and hold people. But the kind and quality of music is likely to be the number one lasting impression people take away from the new service.[6] As Rick Warren, pastor of Saddleback Valley Community Church (Mission Viejo, Calif.), observes, "Music may be the most influential factor in determining who your church reaches for Christ, and whether or not your church grows."[7]

The sermon speaks to the mind; drama speaks to the heart; music speaks to the soul. Ultimately it is the effective interaction of all three that best communicates the message God wants us to share. But music is the key.

I believe that the reason music is such a significant factor in the success of a service is that more than any other communication vehicle, it makes the service indigenous. Music either keeps you out of or invites you into the world of your target audience. Music is the soul language of people. George Hunter observes that "the extent to which the faith is likely indigenized for a given culture is most obviously observed in the church's music, and the people's spontaneous, contagious, celebrative involvement in the music."[8]

How, when, and where music plays a role in your service depends on your target audience and the goal of your service. Here are some generalizations about the role of music and the three variables that define a target audience.

Spiritual Variable

- The more unchurched your target audience, the more they will want to listen to the music. The more churched your target audience, the more they will want to participate in it.
- The more unchurched your target audience, the more the music style (rhythm, beat, instrumentation) should reflect their secular musical preference. The more churched your target audience, the more tolerant they will be of musical variety.

Generational Variable

- The older your target audience, the more important are the words. The younger your target audience, the more important is the rhythm.
- The older the generational group, the mellower the music should be. The younger the group, the harsher the music should be.
- The older the generational group, the longer the same song can be sung or played. The younger the group, the shorter the song should be.

Cultural Variable

- The stronger the cultural identity of your target audience, the more the music should be culturally appropriate. The weaker the cultural identity, the wider the tolerance of music styles.
- The stronger the cultural identity of your target audience, the greater their desire for participation in the music. The weaker the cultural identity, the less desire for participation.

"When we proclaim the gospel in the musical vernacular of those we are trying to reach," notes Dori Collins, "we recover the heritage of one who translated the Bible into the languages of the people, because he understood the power of the vernacular—language that is not apart from, but related to experience."[9]

Musicians

One of the most common obstacles churches encounter when attempting to begin a new style service is finding musicians. The first place most churches look is inward. Are there any musicians in the congregation? That's a natural and reasonable place to begin. But if that well is dry, many are confounded and don't know where to look next. Here are some other sources where churches have found capable musicians:

- Other churches
- Community newspaper classifieds (place an ad or look for an ad)

- High school or college music departments
- Private music teachers and music schools
- Secular and religious music stores
- Music networks (musicians who know other musicians who know other musicians)

Raise the question as to whether you feel that all the musicians must be Christians. Personally, I don't think they need be. In fact, I know of several churches in which the paid musicians came to faith because of their involvement in the service.

The number of musicians on the platform should vary with the size of the congregation. Here are recommended sizes of the total music team (vocal and instrumental) related to congregational size:

Congregational Size	Music Team Size
Less than 50	3
50–100	4–5
100–250	5–6
250–500	6–7
500 or more	7–8

Let's talk briefly about money and music. Specifically, should you pay your musicians? My recommendation is that your music talent be paid. Since the music is the most important part of the service, you should want the best talent possible on your platform. Most larger congregations would have little difficulty finding members willing to donate their time in a musical position, so why not save money and go with volunteers? Here's why I believe you are better off paying your musicians:

- *You have more control.* You tell paid musicians what you want. You ask volunteers what you'd like. People who are paid take orders much more easily.

- *You have more accountability.* You control the time of paid musicians. Volunteers control the time of volunteers. It's not an option for a paid employee to miss a rehearsal and go to the beach.
- *The quality is better.* Paid musicians, as a rule, are more concerned with producing a quality product. Volunteer musicians tend to have lower standards of excellence and demand less of themselves. If the quality of your paid musicians is not up to your standards, you can demand better or dismiss them. Try that with volunteers!
- *Everyone has more tolerance.* A constant leadership challenge in working with volunteers is keeping them happy. And volunteers know (as do you) that if they become unhappy, they can walk. One of the benefits of paid musicians is their greater tolerance of discontentment.

Most churches pay the preacher because they realize that an outstanding sermon requires preparation, practice, and prayer. The same is true for outstanding music. It requires preparation, practice, and prayer.

Music is critical to the success of your new service. As Lyle Schaller suggests, "music is the most influential factor in turning a collection of individuals into a sense of community."[10] It must contribute to the overall message of the service. It must reflect the tastes of the target audience. And it must be good. Give it your best effort.

Drama

Most people think the only kind of service in which drama is appropriate is a contemporary service. Wrong. Drama is a powerful tool in any style of service, with any purpose, for any group. It will help you get across a message in ways that no other communication medium can. There are several reasons that good drama has such powerful impact on people:

170

- It provides a concrete illustration rather than a conceptual description. The power of drama is that in a relatively short period of time you can highlight the key issues and obstacles related to the theme of your service. If the theme is building stronger family relationships, you can visualize the problems of weak families. If the theme is faith, you can illustrate the obstacle of doubt. Drama can isolate issues that are easily clouded by the complexity of the real world.

- It heightens the attention and interest level of the congregation simply through the novelty of the medium. People respond positively to drama, which is the most compelling argument for its use in the church today.[11]

- It is remembered longer, since it involves the visual sense as well as the auditory sense. Educational research has proved that the more senses involved in a learning experience, the more likely the message will be remembered.

Drama can take many forms. Rev. Nancy Goulet, pastor of Epworth United Methodist Church (Kenton, Ohio), delivered a sermon on the woman who touched Jesus' robe. But she "preached" the entire message dressed in the garb common to women of that day, and delivered the entire "sermon" in the first person. She *was* the woman who had just touched Jesus' robe! The congregation was enraptured by the personal story told by the woman who had been healed by the Master.

Sharonville United Methodist (Cincinnati, Ohio) used drama by placing live statues (church members garbed in first-century Roman dress) in the church foyer as part of a series on characters in the New Testament.

The most common use of drama is a three- to five-minute illustration of a key issue related to the message of the service. The most complementary role of drama in a service is to illustrate a problem to which the sermon provides the solution.

Because the medium of drama can be so powerful in helping you communicate your message, I suggest you pay nearly as much attention to finding a good drama coordinator as you do finding a good music director. A well-written, engaging drama will rivet

171

the attention of a congregation. Poorly written or slowly paced drama is an annoying waste of time. "Much amateur drama production suffers from slow pacing," says Steve Pederson.[12] Do it right or don't do it.

You may initially wish to purchase scripts by professional playwrights if you do not have the talent in the church. The Southern Baptist Convention offers a subscription to their *National Drama Service*, a bimonthly publication that provides churches with scripts in a variety of formats.[13] Willow Creek Community Church makes its drama scripts available through Zondervan Publishing House.[14] The Church of the Nazarene publishes a drama catalog that includes a variety of scripts.[15] After a few years, however, most churches find that the drama sketches they write themselves are more useful and relevant to the message they wish to communicate.

An increasing number of seminars, newsletters, and resources are available on drama in the church. The best way to get into the network of people and events in this field is to make friends with someone who coordinates the drama ministry at a creative church in your area.

Storytelling

Memory is not formed from abstract concepts of the mind, but from concrete experiences of the heart. Jesus, of course, was a master storyteller. He knew the indelible place that is created in one's memory by a stimulating, graphic, well-told story. Yet today storytelling has become a lost art. "Storytelling creates community," says Thomas Boomershire. "People who tell each other stories become friends . . . and the deeper the meaning of the story, the deeper the relationships that are formed by the story."[16]

A story is similar to a sermon illustration in that it takes listeners into the realm of their imagination—a powerful and engaging part of the mind. But a story is not a sermon illustration. Whereas a good illustration clarifies a point in the sermon, a good story makes a point that the sermon clarifies. Think about Jesus' parables. Were they sermons or stories? Jesus knew the powerful message that stories could tell and the powerful emotions they could create.

If young families are your target audience, imagine the impact of a series of well-told stories about a family in various life circumstances. If Baby Buster seekers are your target audience, think of the impact of a story chronicling the events leading up to a teen rock star's recent suicide. Stories are most effective when the style and content match the audience.[17]

Storytelling is a skill that can be developed. I recently received a notice from the National Association for the Preservation and Perpetuation of Storytelling[18] inviting me to the National Storytelling Festival. There I could hear and learn to tell ghost stories, family stories, sacred stories, historic stories, and cultural stories. I could receive a bimonthly magazine with how-to articles, stories to use and adapt, and information on how to network with other storytellers.

If you're looking for topics or situations about which you can tell an engaging story, look no farther than the New Testament; some of the best stories have already been told. Simply take a parable and set it in today's context. I recently read a memorable story in a secular magazine that, much to my surprise, turned out to be a modern adaptation of the parable of the prodigal son.

The children's sermon, which often includes an engaging story, is one of the most remembered (by adults) aspects of the entire service. When it comes to effective communication, worship planners do well to learn what works and to do more of it. One thing that works is storytelling. It is fun, engaging, spontaneous, and playful. To say, "Let me tell you a story" is like saying, "Let's go play." Everyone loves a good story.

Puppets

Jim Tippens, pastor of First Baptist Church (Myrtle Beach, S.C.), describes what happened in the middle of a seemingly normal church service recently: "Suddenly, from behind a railing I saw an orange head with a green nose and blue hair. It had the high voice of a child. Every eye in the sanctuary turned to this amazing sight. As the creature began to talk, the congregation became silent. Smiles broke out on people's faces. I could tell that every word was being soaked up by the people."[19] Puppets are becoming increasingly popular in churches that are starting a new service for families. But they need not be limited to family services.

Puppets capture the imagination and produce a sense of child-like innocence in everyone. Puppets can communicate with people in a way other humans cannot. Whereas people are often judged on their appearance, their manner of presentation, or their body language, puppets are immediately accepted. Puppets can easily get the attention of sleepyheaded children and talkative adults. Depending on the script, puppets can teach many moral and spiritual lessons through stories in a way that is reminiscent of Jesus' teaching through parables. Children and adults alike will enjoy and learn through this creative medium.[20]

Multimedia

Adults born prior to 1940 gained most of their knowledge through words. Great preachers, using radio and revivals, built entire ministries on their ability to use words. Indeed, for most of our Christian history, the spoken word (and later printed word) was the only vehicle available to those who wished to pass on the faith.

But in the 1950s, television sets began appearing in homes across America, and the way people learned would change forever. We began to see as well as hear. Baby Boomers became the first generation to be raised on television. And increasingly, as we begin the twenty-first century, we are becoming a visual culture.

What this means, as you begin planning your new service, is that people will be influenced by images of reality more than by descriptions of reality. "We must learn to show, to act out, to paint pictures of, to illuminate the sacred," says Karen Mains.[21] The worship planning team should be looking for multiple ways of communicating God's message on Sunday morning; many of those ways should be visual.

Here are the two primary principles by which people learn:

1. *Redundancy.* People learn when exposed to a message more than one time.
2. *Multisensory.* People learn when exposed to a message in more than one way.

Multimedia simply means using a variety of communication technology for multisensory redundancy. Multimedia in a worship service means a creative combination of media communicating a similar or related message in a different form. Such media can include videotape, overhead projector, posters, audiotape, film, objects, art, slides, noises, smells, or tastes.

Not only is the variety of multimedia important for learning, but in today's media-dominated culture the quality of the media is essential. "Rapidly growing congregations use the most up-to-date technology to enhance the worship mood," notes Howard Griffith. "Hi tech sound systems with a full complement of wireless microphones, mixer boards, tape and CD decks provide the basic tools for sound and music production. To communicate with persons who are more visually-oriented, remote control screens with slide and video projectors and computer support reproduce images ranging from announcements and hymns to biblical scenes, congregational outings, missions projects."[22]

Missionaries frequently use slides or videos to help participants understand life on the other side of the world. A similar technique can help participants understand life on the other side of faith. Christian music videos are increasingly popular and, for certain target groups, can be effective communication devices. Video and film clips from secular Hollywood movies have been effectively used to illustrate issues in a service. Video projectors connected to a personal computer with presentation software can project words to songs in a much more professional manner than overhead projectors.

Pete Ward, pastor of a church in England that began a new service specifically for Baby Busters, describes his church's creative use of visual images: "The modern visual world in which young people live is on the move. In alternative worship, the visual side of Christian worship must also be very much on the move. . . . For example, with a large white sheet and an everyday slide projector we can achieve spectacular visual effects. A picture which is twenty feet high has an amazing impact. Slides allow us to create a sequence of pictures that change throughout the service. Suddenly the visual arts become a responsive, interactive part of our worship."[23]

Creative use of multimedia in your new service will enhance the message by (1) enhancing attention, (2) enhancing involvement, and (3) enhancing retention.

Sermon

The New Testament tells us that preaching is essential to faith, conversion, and Christian growth. "So faith comes from what is heard, and what is heard comes by the preaching of Christ" (Rom. 10:17 RSV). The preached word is a channel through which God, by his Holy Spirit, invites, instructs, challenges, comforts, and energizes people.

Preaching can be high adventure for pastor and congregation alike as the truths of Scripture come alive and are experienced. There are, of course, countless resources, books, tapes, and conferences on preaching. In this limited context, I would like to share with you a technique that Joe Harding, one of my favorite preachers, uses for experiencing Scripture, which he then shares with his congregation on Sunday morning:

> Because Scripture deals primarily with God's action in history, there is invariably a meaningful picture to be seen in the text. The picture may be immediately evident in the passage or it may reveal itself more reluctantly. Somewhere, however, there will be a picture. The preacher needs to see it and then imaginatively enter it.
>
> In your imagination observe the persons involved in the text. What are they doing? What is the situation they face? How do they feel? What are their problems? What are their desires?
>
> It's helpful to me to move inside the text and begin to look around from several different perspectives. I imagine myself as a

176

film director coming in for close-up shots of different people and places in the story. What sounds do we hear? What do we smell? What do we feel as we imaginatively touch the people and objects in the situation? What emotions are stirred as we listen and watch? View one person in this way, then another.

The experience we have as we step into this biblical story may carry an obvious meaning and need little comment. Or it may lend itself to a parallel presentation of a contemporary picture and story. There may be moments where you and the congregation stand aside from the story to look at its meaning and implication. The story may be occasionally shared in the first person. It may be from the perspective of the writer standing off on the side observing the proceedings. It may be from a minor personality who appears in the story.

It is critical that every sermon move from the Scriptural story to the story of today . . . to the earthy, specific, recognizable events and needs in the everyday world of the listener. Harry Emerson Fosdick places a great emphasis on the intersection of life situations and Biblical truth when he recommends that "every sermon should have for its main business the head-on constructive meeting of some problem which is puzzling minds, burdening consciences, distracting lives. And no sermon which so meets a real human difficulty, with light to throw on it and help to win a victory over it, could possibly be futile."

As we experience the story, sermon preparation is therefore not the memorization of words from a manuscript. Preparation is a revisiting and clarifying of the story and its message morning after morning. By the time Sunday arrives, the story has been visualized and experienced vividly a number of times. Standing before the congregation you are free of notes, free to move, free to experience, free to share, free to weep or rejoice, and finally free by tone and body language to say non-verbally: "this is really *true!* It is true for me. I know the reality of which I speak. My life is already changed!"[24]

A sample sermon by Dr. Harding is included in appendix D as an illustration of the principles of sharing the story of the gospel.

Testimonies

A true-life story is one of the most powerful means of touching someone's mind and heart. Good communicators know that when they illustrate a point with a true story of a changed life it can have a dramatic impact on the listener, particularly if the subject is known to the listener.

But great communicators know that when the subject tells his or her own story, the impact can be far greater than that of a secondhand recounting. The power of a personal testimony is awesome. If indeed the service is the message (rather than the sermon), a personal testimony can be one of the best "messages" you can share with your congregation.

Rev. Nancy Goulet preached a sermon in the Sharonville United Methodist Church (Cincinnati, Ohio) on why bad things happen to good people. As part of the sermon, she had a member of the church share his personal thoughts and feelings on what life had been like for him during the past year since being diagnosed with cancer. The clear and heartfelt testimony that the man shared made Rev. Goulet's sermon sing with reality.

Testimonies can also be shared through dialogue between the subject and an interviewer (the pastor or worship leader). This makes it easier for laypeople, who may not be accustomed to speaking in public, to share their story. Developing the questions and reviewing them with the subject ahead of time allows for a comfortable and interesting time of sharing a personal and often moving story.

Bringing the Ingredients Together

After the planning of a meaningful, effective, communicative service, the worship planning team still has one important challenge—the mix. Bringing all the ingredients together into a smoothly flowing, well-paced experience will make your service breathe of quality. And to the worshipers a quality service communicates a quality God.

178

Rehearse the Service

Most churches that do an exceptional job of presenting a quality worship experience have at least one complete rehearsal of the entire service. They have learned the paradox of presenting a quality service: The more you rehearse the service, the more spontaneous it appears. The converse is also true: The less you prepare, the less natural the service appears.

I strongly suggest you rehearse every service prior to each Sunday, even after you have several dozen services under your belt. Don't become complacent. Each service is a new and dynamic experience.

One element to pay particular attention to in your rehearsal is pace. In a church service, seventy-five minutes can seem like twenty minutes, and twenty minutes can seem like seventy-five. The difference is pace. "Most church services move at a snail's pace," observes Rick Warren.[25] The pacing goal for your service is to leave people surprised that the service is over, not relieved.

Television has forever changed the attention span of Americans. The average length between commercials is now down to seven minutes. MTV has shortened the attention span of Baby Busters even more. In one three-minute video alone you may be bombarded with several thousand images. "A persuasive argument can be made," observes Lyle Schaller, "that the most significant single influence of television on churches has been to teach people to expect a fast-paced presentation."[26]

A variety of things will improve the pace of your service:

- Use multiple platform personalities.
- Avoid singing three to five verses of the same song.
- Keep pastoral prayers short.
- Reduce announcements to a minute or less.
- Move smoothly and swiftly from one activity to the next.
- Avoid dead space (fill the space with a musical bridge).
- Keep the sermon under twenty minutes.
- Include a variety of communication mediums.

Incidentally, here's a new insight I discovered in researching churches that were successfully offering multiple services: Those leading the worship service are not there primarily to worship. Rather, they are there to lead others to worship. The personal time of worship among those on the platform should be some other time in the day or week, not during the service.

The Critical Ingredient

The Simi Valley Covenant Church (Simi Valley, Calif.) has an intercessory prayer team that arrives at the church early on Sunday morning to pray. They go to each classroom and pray for the teacher who will be teaching there. Then they go to each seat in the auditorium and pray for the person who will be sitting there. Pastor Kurt Frederickson pointedly observes of this growing church, "After all the fun and games, it's prayer that moves this church forward."[27]

Christ United Methodist Church (Nashville, Tenn.) has three services on a weekend. While each service is going on, there is a group of people at prayer for the pastor, the worship team, and the people in that service.

Prayer is a powerful and critical ingredient in the success of your new service. In fact, I suggest that you establish a worship prayer team for your new service. This group's sole purpose is to ask God to be powerfully present in the service, and to ask his healing touch on the lives of those present. Here is a list of prayer suggestions for such a group:

- Pray for the worship planning team.
- Pray for the people in attendance.
- Pray for the pastor.
- Pray for special needs that arise related to the service.
- Pray for the worship leaders.
- Pray for the hosts and greeters in the service.
- Pray for the lay leaders teaching Sunday school and helping out in the nursery during the service.

- Pray for the presence of the Holy Spirit.
- Pray for the conversion of unreached men and women.

The power of praying for, and being prayed for, is life changing. Bathe your new service (and all your present services, for that matter) with petitions to God for his presence and blessing. Then do all you can to fulfill your responsibility of planning, preparing, and presenting a service that God can use.

In the next chapter we'll talk about the important steps in getting enough people at the service in order to establish the core group that will ensure momentum from day one.

Getting People to Come

Your new service is planned. It is a model of creative outreach to people you are presently not reaching. You've designed a series of services that present your message in a relevant and meaningful manner. The service time and location are the best choices, based on your research. The music fits the style and tastes of your target audience. Everything seems right for exciting new ministry and outreach to begin.

But what if no one shows up?

Let's consider how to get the word out to initially attract enough people for the service to develop its own momentum and become self-sustaining.

What Is Your Starting Size?

Here's an axiom that explains much of the growth of today's megachurches. It affects the success of your new service, as well: *Crowds attract crowds.*

If too few people are present in the first four to six meetings of your new service, two things will occur: (1) those who do attend will conclude that it must not be a quality experience, since not many others are attending; (2) those who did the work of preparing for (and who took a risk for) the new service will become discouraged with what appears to be the makings of a failure. Obviously, neither is desirable.

Don't plan for your new service to start small and get bigger. Plan to start big and get bigger. While you aren't necessarily trying to start a megaservice, you are trying to start a service that will be around for a while. And that requires beginning with a *critical mass.*

The critical mass for your new service is the number of people necessary to grow beyond the first six months. It is comparable to a rocket ship having enough fuel to launch it out of earth's gravity and into outer space. A critical mass in your service is necessary for survival because there is a predictable attendance pattern that you will encounter in the first year. It looks something like figure 31.

Figure 31

Common Attendance Pattern in First Year of New Service

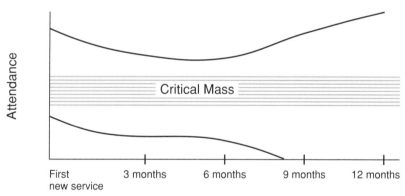

The top line illustrates attendance at a new service that began above its critical mass and did not descend below it during the first six months. The lower line illustrates attendance at a new service that started below, and never reached, its critical mass. It is also possible, of course, for a new service to start above and descend below, or start below and ascend above, its critical mass.

184

What to Expect in the First Six Months

Most new services experience an initial decline in attendance (often up to 25 percent) during the first several months, after which they often plateau for several months. If your new service begins at or above your critical mass—and stays there for the first six months—you are safe in assuming that you have weathered the most perilous time in the life of the service. If, on the other hand, your service begins below, or drops below, the critical mass in the first six months, there is often insufficient energy for the service to begin growing again, and it will probably die.

Among the churches I have studied that began a new service and canceled it within the first year, almost 85 percent began below, or descended below, their critical mass in the first six months.

Here are two other important observations about critical mass: (1) the sooner you reach it, the more rapid will be your subsequent growth; (2) the longer it takes to reach it, the lower the attendance level at which your service will plateau. (And, if you recall the discussion on life cycles, all services eventually plateau.)

The long-term (two- to three-year) growth potential of your new service is strongly affected by the time it takes to reach your critical mass. The relationship is illustrated in figure 32.

Figure 32

Growth Potential and Critical Mass

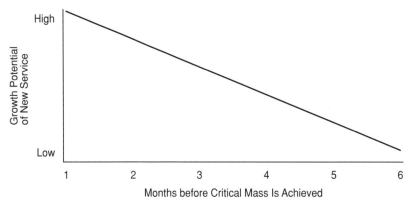

Months before Critical Mass Is Achieved

What Is Your Critical Mass?

"So," you are probably saying, "what is the critical mass we need for our new service?" Unfortunately it is not one simple number that applies to all services. The critical mass is a factor of two numbers: (1) the attendance of your present largest service, and (2) your meeting room size.

Based on my studies of successful and unsuccessful new services, there is a certain minimum threshold that you should attain to be assured of reaching your critical mass. This number reflects average attendance during the first six weeks. If you reach it within this time, you will be at or above the critical mass necessary to weather a 20 to 25 percent decline in the first three months and still have an adequate nucleus for eventual growth.

Attendance goal 1: At least fifty people or 35 percent of your largest present service, whichever is greater. Fifty people seems to be the minimum number for insuring a successful new service, regardless of any other variable. To put it simply, most new services that begin with less than fifty people don't survive the first year. Most new services that begin with more than fifty people do survive.

Attendance goal 2: At least 35 percent of those in attendance should be previously unchurched or inactive. In most cases this will be easy. You'll find that if your new service is focused on a new target group, and if you've designed an adequate communication strategy to reach these people, 65 percent or more of those in attendance will be unchurched or inactive. The minimum goal of 35 percent also prevents a musical chairs process of simply moving your present congregation from one service to another.

Room capacity goal: The meeting room should be filled to at least 50 percent capacity. It is far better to bring in more chairs and squeeze into a small room than to have many empty chairs or pews and get lost in a big room. This is one reason, as we discussed earlier, that it may be better to meet in a facility other than your sanctuary.

Figure 33 translates the above goals into specific numbers related to the size of your largest service and the ideal room capacity.

Figure 33

Attendance and Room Capacity Goals for Your New Service

Attendance at Your Present Largest Service	Attendance Goal for New Service within 6 Weeks	Unchurched or Inactive Goal for New Service	Ideal Meeting Room Seating Capacity
Less than 50	50	17	66–77
50–100	50	17	66–77
100–150	52	17	69–80
150–200	70	24	93–108
200–250	87	30	116–134
250–300	105	37	140–161
300–400	140	49	187–215
400–500	175	61	233–269
500–750 or more	262	92	349–403

In the remainder of this chapter we will discuss how to reach your critical mass in the initial weeks of your new service.

How to Get a Crowd

To see significant numbers of new people in your new service, you must do two things: (1) communicate with your target audience so they are aware of the new service—an "exposure" issue; (2) convince your target audience that they should attend—a "perceived value" issue.

You have two vehicles available to accomplish these objectives: (1) personal invitations and (2) public announcements. The order in which I've listed these two communication vehicles is not random. The first vehicle is the more effective way of communicating with your target audience.

So what kind of response rate can you expect from the people who hear about your new service? Here are figures that present a relatively accurate way to project the response rate of those who receive your invitation to attend the new service (in other words, how many will show up):

Type of Communication	Positive Response Rate
Personal Invitation	10–25%
Public Announcement	$\frac{1}{4}$–2%

A personal invitation is an invitation from one person to another (face to face or by telephone); the two individuals know each other. A public announcement can be a newspaper ad, direct mail, radio or television spot, a telemarketing campaign, posters, door hangers, and so on.

If your response rates are lower than indicated in the chart above, the communication strategy did not convince your target audience that the benefit of attending was worth the cost.

With this information, you can generally evaluate your communication strategy and project the results. For example, suppose your goal is 100 people at your first new service. If you put all your eggs in the personal invitation basket, your strategy would be to extend 400 to 1,000 personal invitations, which should result in at least 100 people attending, assuming a 10 to 25 percent response rate.

If, however, you were to focus entirely on public advertising to generate the crowd, your strategy would be to contact 5,000 to 40,000 people through a public announcement, which should also result in at least 100 people, assuming a $\frac{1}{4}$ to 2 percent response rate.

Of course, there are many variations on the use of these two communication vehicles that will also attract 100 people. Figure 34 presents some other examples.

In considering your long-term strategy for growth of the new service, I suggest you place the greater emphasis on personal invitations for several reasons:

- There will be a significantly higher visitor return rate in subsequent weeks among those who attend your new service

Figure 34

How to Attract One Hundred People to Your First New Service

	Projected Response Rate	Example 1		Example 2		Example 3	
		No. of Contacts	No. of Responses	No. of Contacts	No. of Responses	No. of Contacts	No. of Responses
Personal Invitation	15%	333	**50**	500	**75**	167	**25**
Public Announcement	³/₄%	6,700	**50**	3,350	**25**	10,000	**75**
Total			**100**		**100**		**100**

because of the invitation of a friend. Conversely, fewer visitors who came in response to a public announcement will return.

- Over the long term, you have greater growth potential among those who came in response to a personal invitation. People invited by a friend are more likely to invite a friend on their own, whereas those who came because of a public announcement assume that others will begin attending for the same reason they did. Personal invitations allow for a process of multiplication (as friends invite friends who invite friends); public announcements are simply a process of addition. (For a comprehensive discussion and outreach strategy based on this network principle, see *The Master's Plan for Making Disciples* by Win and Charles Arn.)[1]

- You will see fewer dropouts in the first year among those who originally began attending because of a personal invitation, compared with those who began attending in response to a public announcement.

- Personal invitations are a much more cost-efficient means of reaching your critical mass.

- Personal invitations involve existing members in the outreach process and help them grow in their own spiritual lives. Not so with public announcements.

189

- When unchurched friends and family members begin attending, there is greater enthusiasm and support for the new service throughout the congregation.

Despite the fact that the long-term growth of your new service should be built around personal invitations, experience indicates that during the first few months, most of those attending (other than your own members) will come because of public announcements. Most members won't invite a friend until they see what's going on for themselves and are convinced that the quality of the new service will be consistently high. If you do have a high-quality service, the number of members inviting friends will grow. The common pattern can be seen in figure 35.

Figure 35

Source of Newcomers* in a New Service

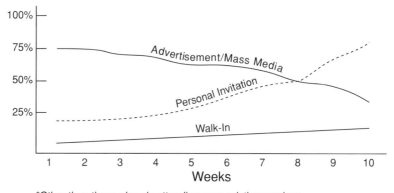

*Other than those already attending your existing services

Planning Your Communication Strategy

Developing and implementing an effective communication strategy is an important part of your growth mix. All your research, planning, and persuasive energy will go for naught if no one shows up at the new service. For this reason, I recommend you recruit a group of laypeople to serve on a communications task force.

190

Their responsibility is to get the word out, which includes both a personal invitation strategy and a public announcement strategy. Because the public announcement strategy is more involved and costly, several of the members of the group should have experience in advertising. People employed in this field often enjoy applying their knowledge and skills to creatively promoting the new service.

Some of the following material may sound like marketing to you. Before jumping to the conclusion that this is bad, let me share with you a generally accepted definition of marketing: "Learning the needs of the customer and then providing a product or service to meet those needs, delivering it in an appropriate way in the appropriate time, place, and context."[2]

You are hopefully filling a need in people's lives with a genuine quality "product." If you don't like the term marketing, fine. Call it whatever you wish. But the concern is to communicate the value of your new church service to your target audience in a way that will motivate them to act differently—namely, to go to church.

In the remainder of this chapter we will discuss the two communication vehicles through which invitations can be extended to your target audience.

Personal Invitation

As mentioned earlier, personal invitation is the method of preference for growing your new service. It is cheaper than public announcements, it is less risky, it has a higher response rate, it involves more members, creates greater ownership, and results in a higher percentage of returning visitors. On top of all that, it's easier.

Your goal should be to see approximately 20 percent of those in your existing service extend a personal invitation to a friend, relative, or associate to visit the new service. Here are some suggestions for your communications committee to see this goal realized:

1. If you want a significant number of your members to invite a friend to the new service, personally ask them to do so. Face-to-face or telephone requests are far superior to notices in the bulletin, suggestions in the church newsletter, or public announcements to "bring a friend." Here is the insight, whether you are recruiting for a church role, soliciting for a special project, asking for prayer, or encouraging members to bring a friend to church: People respond to personal requests, not impersonal requests.

2. Print a one-page flyer about the new service. Give a brief description of the service, including the purpose, the target audience, the kind of music, and the themes that will be addressed. Include a map on the back with the time and location of the service.

Next make a list of the church leadership boards, committees, small groups, classes, and other regular gatherings of members. At these meetings distribute four copies of the flyer to each person in attendance. Explain that new services grow through invitations to friends and family. Ask these leaders to write down the name of two to four people they know who might be interested in attending the new service. Then ask them to give one copy of the flyer to each of these people and extend a personal invitation. If some of the groups meet weekly (such as Sunday school classes), hand out copies of the flyer each week for four to six weeks prior to the first new service.

3. Conduct a sample of the new service so members who are considering inviting a friend will know what to expect. Most people won't invite a friend to a service unless they are fairly sure of what will happen and decide it will not jeopardize their relationship.

If you conduct a sample service, I strongly suggest you do not replace a regularly scheduled service with the new service, even for one Sunday. Rather, give members a choice of whether to attend the sample service. Perhaps sponsor a churchwide dinner or picnic before or after the sample service so you can communicate the motive and rationale for the service.

Prior to the service distribute a handout that reviews the stated purpose of the church and how this new style service relates to that purpose. Include a description of the target audience and the goal of the new service. The handout should also describe the components of the new service and why each element is included. Focus on the goal: touching people for Christ who would not otherwise be reached.

Offer a short feedback session at the conclusion of the service for any members who would like to ask questions. The reason for this forum is not necessarily to solicit suggestions; in most cases members who are comfortable with "their own" service will have few suggestions for the new service. Rather, the feedback time is to give people a chance to share their comments with you up front instead of complaining later behind your back.

4. *Four weeks prior to the new service, personally ask members for names and addresses of friends and family who do not attend church.* Tell members that you would like to send these people a flyer, and later a postcard, announcing the new service. Explain that the information will be sent from the church and that members' names will not be used. It is helpful to show the postcard or brochure to members prior to asking for names.

5. *Include a blank space in the church bulletin for members to write the names and addresses of people they know who would benefit from attending the new service.* Do this on each of the four Sundays prior to launching the new service. Allow two to three minutes during the regular service for members to write the information and to pray silently for these people. Close this time with a public prayer restating the church's commitment to reach out to those outside the church and ask for God's blessing in this step of faith.

6. *Print a three-by-five-inch card to insert in the church bulletin the two Sundays prior to the new service.* The card could look something like figure 36.

Point out the card during these two services and ask members to complete the card and keep it with them as a reminder to invite those people in the coming week. Share the fact that 75 to 90 percent of those who begin attending church do so because of the invitation of a friend or relative. You could also refer to the research that indicates approximately 35 percent of unchurched people said they would attend church if invited by a friend. This same

Figure 36

> When I think about the people God has placed in my life who are not presently active in a local church, I think he would have me invite the following two people to our new service:
>
> _____
> _____
> _____
> _____
> _____

three-by-five-inch card should be distributed in the sample service mentioned earlier.

Public Announcement

While personal invitations are the most fruitful and cost-effective means of growing your new service, it will take several months before people are regularly inviting others. As a result, attendance of newcomers for the first several months will be largely dependent on your public announcement strategy.

As you begin to formulate your public announcement strategy, remember two basic principles about mass marketing:

1. Say it more than one time. There is one principle that works above all others: Redundancy. Redundancy. Redundancy. Redundancy. Redundancy. Studies of retention tell us that people can hear the same message up to seven different times and learn something new each time. That is why you see television commercials repeated so often. The implication for your new service: Communicate with your target audience five to seven different times.

2. Say it more than one way. The more senses involved in receiving your message, the more likely your message will be remembered. People who only hear a message will remember less than those who hear and see it. That is why television ads are considerably more expensive than radio—advertisers know they sell more through a multisensory medium. The implication for your new service: Use a variety of media to communicate with your target audience.

Review Your Target Audience

One additional word of advice before you leap into the world of Madison Avenue: Know your target audience. The members of the communications committee, who will be developing the promotion for the new service, should meet with those who were involved in the target group research. If focus groups were conducted, the summary of major findings should be carefully reviewed. Be certain that the communications task force has a clear understanding of the defining issues of your target audience.

Where Are Your Prospects?

An ancient proverb can help improve your marketing strategy for the new service: The more places you search for fish, the more likely you will find dinner.

List all the different places where your target audience will be found. Even though you are focusing on just one "people group," these individuals will be found in a number of different places. Here are some "pools" where you will find "fish" receptive to your message. They are presented in a hierarchy of receptiveness—more respondents will come from the initial groups listed:

1. *Existing members' friends and relatives who do not attend church.* This will be one of your most receptive pools within your target audience. And the response rate will be particularly high if your public announcement strategy complements your personal invitation strategy. New Christians in particular will have a large number of unchurched friends and relatives.
2. *Visitors who have not returned.* Most churches find that only 10 to 12 percent of their visitors eventually become members. This means that nearly 90 percent of the visitors didn't

come back. If you have a method of obtaining names and addresses of visitors (and you should), extend an invitation to these folks to try your new service. Many will.

3. *Programs and special ministries of the church.* Participants of special interest groups, support groups, recreational groups, and recovery groups that meet in your facility (church sponsored or not) are composed of people familiar with your church building. If the church has a television, radio, or literature ministry, the people whose names are acquired through this outreach should receive an invitation as well.

4. *Inactive members of your church.* People who have left a church will sometimes return if there is a significant change of some kind in the church. The longer a person has been gone, the more difficult it is for the person to return. But a new service often provides an excellent reason to try again.

5. *Christmas and Easter visitors.* The joke about the church's annual attendance graph looking like a two-humped camel is too often true—the humps being Christmas and Easter. But if you have a way of obtaining names and addresses of holiday visitors, these people are good prospects to try your new service.

6. *Wedding and funeral contacts.* This group includes the couples married in your church, as well as their friends and families. Widows, widowers, and extended families affected by a funeral conducted by the pastor will be receptive to your invitation. A personal phone call or visit by the pastor (or officiating staff person) will be far more effective than a letter or flyer.

7. *Families of children who were involved in your summer vacation Bible school.* An invitation to your new service is an excellent reason to contact this receptive group of people.

8. *People in transition.* Research has shown that individuals in a condition of life transition are more likely to change their religious behavior—specifically, from not going to church, to doing so.[3] The Holmes-Rahe Social Readjustment Scale (fig. 37) is a valuable tool for identifying people in transition who are often experiencing a vacuum that God's love

196

Figure 37

Holmes-Rahe Social Readjustment Scale

Death of spouse 100
Divorce 73
Marital separation 65
Death of close family member 63
Jail term 63
Severe personal injury or illness 53
Marriage 50
Fired from work 47
Marital reconciliation 45
Retirement 45
Change in family member's health 44
Pregnancy 40
Sex difficulties 39
Addition to family 39
Business readjustment 39
Change in financial status 38
Death of close friend 37
Change in number of marital arguments 35
Mortgage or loan over $75,000 31
Foreclosure on mortgage 30
Change in work responsibilities 29
Son or daughter leaves home 29
Trouble with in-laws 29
Outstanding personal achievement 28
Spouse starts work 26
Start or finish school 26
Change in living conditions 25
Revision of personal habits 24
Trouble with boss 23
Change in work hours/conditions 20
Change in residence 20
Change in recreational habits 19
Change in social activities 18
Mortgage or loan under $75,000 18
Easter season 17
Change in sleeping habits 16
Change in number of family gatherings 15
Vacation 13
Christmas 12
Minor violation of the law 11

could fill. The numbers to the right of each event indicate the relative significance of the event on a scale of 100. Events that occur in proximity compound a person's stress.

9. *Inactive members of other churches.* This has been a source of growth for many new services. If these people are inactive in their faith and have not been to church in quite a while, you should feel no guilt or remorse in welcoming them into an active church community.

The Four Ps of Marketing

Regardless of the media you use in your public announcement strategy, the message needs to be convincing. Percentages given earlier about the response rate to mass media ($1/4$ percent to 2 percent) assume a quality ad presenting a product (your new service) that is perceived to fulfill a felt need in the target audience. Advertising that is not well conceived or well presented does nothing but waste money. In some cases it is even harmful if it unintentionally communicates an undesirable message about your church.

One approach to developing an effective public announcement strategy is to work through the four Ps of marketing. When you can adequately identify and describe each P, you are well on your way to designing an effective strategy.[4]

1. *Product.* What is your product? What do you offer the consumer to satisfy his or her perceived need?
2. *Place.* In what context or place is your product delivered? How do you get your product to the people you are trying to serve?
3. *Promotion.* What means do you use for communicating the nature and availability of your product to your target audience? Is it the most effective communication strategy for these people?
4. *Price.* What is the cost that the consumer is being asked to pay for your product? Does the consumer perceive the benefit to be worth the price?

Wrestling with these important questions will put your communications task force in the shoes of the "consumer"—those you are trying to reach. It's easy to slip into the trap of saying, "We have the answer. You come and get it, on our terms, at our time, on our turf." Taking the four Ps approach will help you start from their point of view and answer the question, How is the gospel good news in light of their perceived needs, concerns, situation, and preoccupations?

What Advertising Will and Won't Do

It's important to understand the strengths and weaknesses of church advertising. There are some things that effective ads can do, and there are some things they can't do.

A good ad will not:

- *convert people.* Even the best ad will not convince many people, if any, to come to faith. Research found long ago that media campaigns are ineffective for conversion growth.[5] People become Christians through the influence of those they trust.
- *replace experience.* Even the best advertisement cannot change reality. People ultimately respond to the experience they have in your church, not the experience that is promised. Be sure first-time visitors leave with a positive memory and a desire to return for more. Only advertise what you can deliver.

A good ad will:

- *attract visitors.* An effective ad will increase the number of people who try your new service for the first time. If your goal is to increase the number of visitors who "sample your product," a good series of ads can help.
- *create image.* A good ad will position your church and new service in the minds of your community. Image is an important part of whether people decide to try your church. A

199

series of upbeat, positive, creative advertisements will communicate that here is a church in touch with the times.

* *raise congregational self-esteem.* In education and business they call this the self-fulfilling prophecy. For your church, it means that when members see the creative ads about the new service and hear the promise of something special, they feel better about themselves and what their church has to offer.

Media for Your Public Announcement

You will eventually need to determine the media available for your advertising, those best suited for your needs, and the ones that are most cost-effective. "In general, radio and television are most effective in communicating a message built around a personality," observes Lyle Schaller. "By contrast, direct mail is most effective when the message is designed specifically and precisely in response to the unmet needs of the recipient. Newspaper advertisements tend to be most effective in communicating the idea that a particular congregation is composed of 'people pretty much like ourselves.'"[6]

Remember the communication principle: Say it more than one way. Plan on more than one medium for your public announcement strategy.

The planning chart in figure 38 may help you identify and organize your communication strategy.

Here are a few suggestions on the use of various media.

Direct Mail

* For maximum readership, use a stamp on the envelope rather than metered or bulk rate. (Bulk-rate, nonprofit stamps are available from the post office.)
* Address the envelope by hand.
* If you are mailing a flyer, include a cover letter.
* Write the copy in a personable, readable, honest style.

200

Figure 38

Communication Planning Chart

Target Audience: _____

Communication Strategy	Personal Invitation (Check One)	Public Announcement	Things to Do	By When	Who Is Responsible	Budget

- Mail more than once; different people will respond to the second mailing than to the first, even when the mailings are identical.
- Send a last-minute postcard to arrive the week before your new service.

A helpful book on this topic is *Direct Mail Ministry* by Walter Mueller.[7]

Telephone

- Contact your local phone company for help installing temporary lines ("phone bank") to make the calls over a two-week period from the church.
- Plan to make several thousand phone calls.

- Prepare a written script and train the callers.
- Ask people you call if they would like to receive more information on the new service (approximately 10 percent will say yes).
- Your goal for the phone calls is to add people to your mailing list, not to get commitments to attend the service.

Calvary Baptist Church (Las Cruces, N.M.) conducted a citywide telemarketing campaign to launch its new Saturday night service. "We made 19,000 calls and put 1,300 names on a mailing list," says Josh Hunt, associate pastor. About 125 attended on opening night." This process was supplemented by moving a core group of people from their Sunday morning worship service.[8]

A helpful resource for organizing and training people for a phone campaign is *Calling in Love*.[9]

Newspaper Ads

- Focus on and write copy toward your target audience.
- Highlight relationships and people, not programs and institutions.
- No more than 40 percent of the ad should be copy; most of the ad should be title, picture, or white space.
- Advertise on Wednesday for any events the following Sunday.
- Place the ad where your target audience will be reading; avoid the church page.
- Develop a series of ads with the same format but with variations in message.
- Run the ads weekly.
- Use the local paper, not the metropolitan paper.
- Articles (written by newspaper staff reporters) are as valuable as paid ads; make friends with the religion editor.

A catalog of creative church ads is available upon request from the Church Ad Project.[10]

Radio and Television

- Get information about audience profiles of radio and TV stations in your area; use only stations and/or programs that reach your target audience.
- Hire a professional advertising agency to develop the spots.
- Focus on and write copy toward your target audience.
- Offer a gift related to your target audience to increase the number of listeners who respond.
- Don't expect listeners to remember a seven-digit phone number. Get a phone number with letters that form a word (i.e., NEW-LIFE, or 292-LOVE).

A helpful book for your communications task force to read is *Promotion Strategies for the Local Church* by Wayne Kiser.[11]

Using Existing Members

Many churches that have successfully added a new service have "seeded" the service with their own people. This is a good idea. In this process, members volunteer to attend the new service for the first six weeks to help reach the critical mass and get the new service off the ground. These people are "short-term missionaries," giving their time and support to a new outreach initiative. Doug Murren writes, "Before starting a new service, sell the idea to a core of sixty to two hundred people (depending on your size)."[12]

Bethany Lutheran Church (Slidel, La.) began a Sunday evening alternative service and enlisted 18 families (64 people) to temporarily change their worship and Sunday school time to Sunday evening. Another 28 members indicated they would attend on a regular basis. The first service began with 87 people (76 members and 11 visitors) and has grown to 226 regular attenders.

Ascension Lutheran Church (Thousand Oaks, Calif.) asked 75 members from its three Sunday services to attend the new Saturday night service during the first several months. The service now averages over 100 people, most of whom are newcomers.

If you decide to ask some of your members to be "missionaries" to the new service, don't just encourage people to attend. Make a list of those who agree to attend. Leadership Network suggests securing from members a written commitment to attend the new service: "With signed commitments a church will know something of the regular attendance before it begins."[13] If members can't or won't attend all six of the first services, ask them for the dates they will be there.

Set a goal of having 20 percent of those who attend your present service commit to being a missionary for the first six weeks of the new service. These people should be encouraged to continue attending the existing service during those six weeks or you will have a 20 percent drop in attendance in that service.

Plan on "Defectors"

It is not uncommon for a new service to siphon attenders from the present service. First Baptist Church (Forest Grove, Oreg.) was averaging 250 in its one, relatively traditional service. Six months later, after adding a second, more contemporary service, the church was averaging 225 in the contemporary service but only 70 in the traditional service. Despite the total attendance increase of nearly 20 percent, the folks in the traditional service were unhappy that "their" service had become so poorly attended. And why shouldn't they be? It's much more enjoyable worshiping in a full sanctuary than an empty one.

It is helpful to realize on the front end that your new service will not be attended exclusively by your target audience. Even the most seeker-targeted services are significantly attended by believers. Services targeted at Baby Boomers will attract older adults. Some will prefer the relevance of the topics. Others will find the time of day preferable. Still others will be attracted to the music. In any case, don't worry about it. Most churches that add an additional service find that 10 to 20 percent of their present attenders move to the new service periodically or permanently. This is the most important reason why it is critical to keep the quality of the existing service(s) at or above where it was before the new service was added.

If your attendance drop is greater than 20 percent, the reason is probably that many people who attended your existing service(s) were rather dissatisfied. Consider yourself lucky to have discovered this widespread attitude and offered a more attractive alternative before their dissatisfaction turned to departure. In any case, when those who prefer the original service(s) see people "defecting," they will need a particularly strong dose of TLC, and assurance that their service will not be discontinued.

One good way to accommodate the drop in attendance of your existing service(s) is to adjust the seating (if you have movable chairs) to accommodate fewer people. Remember that the perceived "fullness" of a room is greatly related to the room setup. You can adjust a room to look fuller by spreading out chairs, increasing space between rows, and putting fewer chairs in rows. By doing so you will help ease the jolt that may be felt when attendance in the present service(s) drops because of the new service.

In Conclusion

The time and effort you spend on generating critical mass is an important step in successfully starting a new service. Plan ahead. Use your best creative volunteer talent. Buy the marketing wisdom you may not have. Put the necessary effort and money into getting people to try your new service. And if you have a genuine need-meeting service, your rocket ship will be off the launching pad and heading out on an exciting stellar journey.

Evaluating
the Service

~

Your first service is over! After months of praying, preparing, planning, and promoting, everyone involved heaves a collective sigh of relief. Your accomplishment was Herculean, perhaps even miraculous. Congratulations! You deserve a break.

Oops! Not quite yet, sorry. There's another critical step—evaluation. Immediately evaluating the first service is essential to its short- and long-term growth. Everyone who had a part in planning or presenting the service should attend the evaluation session, along with five or six people who had no personal involvement. Meet for no more than an hour and cover the following agenda:

Item 1: Genuinely thank those people who had a part in the preparation or presentation of the new service. Try to mention each person by name and state the role he or she had. (As opposed to saying, "Thanks to everyone who had a part.")

Item 2: Take a moment to pray and thank God for his presence in the intervening months and for the success of simply arriving at this point. Ask for his blessing and wisdom as the new service develops its unique character.

Item 3: Ask for general comments. The pastor should share his or her thoughts first, then others should be asked for their

207

overall assessment. Don't get overly specific at this time; that will come later. Just solicit general perceptions of how the first service went.

Item 4: Review the goal of the new service as defined early in the process. Ask people to comment on whether they felt this goal was reached and to give reasons for their comments.

Item 5: Review the service in detail. Discuss each part of the service, including content, logistics, sound, lighting, transitions, and delivery. Ask people to share what they liked, as well as what they thought could be done better next time.

Begin by reviewing what happened during the five to ten minutes prior to the service. Next review the opening, how the service actually began. Then progress through each activity of the service. Keep the discussion and evaluation objective so people do not feel they are being personally critiqued. Include the sermon in the evaluation process as well. Review such things as relevance, persuasiveness, length, and illustrations. (Pastor: Don't be defensive.) Finally, review the closing of the service—the last thing people heard or experienced before they left.

The first several months of your new service is a unique window of opportunity for you to make changes before you develop a tradition. Hylyard Irvin, pastor of Glendale First Church of the Nazarene (Glendale, Ariz.), shares his firsthand experience: "It is imperative that you remain flexible in the transition to a new service. Don't be afraid of 'reverse gear.' If you find out something is not working, get out of it and change."[1] One of the most refreshing things about starting a new service is that no one can say, "We've never done it that way before."

Evaluating Attendance

I like the comment by Donald McGavran, who said, "Numbers give us an indication of how vital and valid our ministry is. And there is nothing particularly spiritual in not counting."[2]

In evaluating attendance at your new service there are two important questions to ask:

1. Was attendance at or above critical mass? Compare the attendance at this service with the goals suggested in chapter 8. As noted earlier, establishing a critical mass will be important early in the life of the new service to allow you to weather the decline in attendance that is likely to come. If it appears that you have an attractive service but that insufficient numbers of invitations were extended to draw the desired crowd, call an emergency meeting for the coming week with the communcations task force to get the word out about the new service. Don't wait and hope that word spreads on its own.

2. Are we reaching our intended target audience? Despite your best research, your most creative marketing, and your most inspiring message, it is quite possible that although your new service will begin to attract people, they will not be the ones you originally intended.

The Pasadena (Calif.) Church of the Nazarene discovered that its new 9:00 service was being well received and was growing. But while it was originally designed to be a seeker-targeted service, those attending were predominantly believers.

A Presbyterian church in Oregon found that while the goal in adding a new contemporary service at 9:00 was to attract young adults, "it ended up with all the Democrats coming to the first service and the Republicans coming at 11:00."[3]

The decision about what to do with a service that is attracting people other than your intended target audience is fairly simple. If total attendance of all services combined has increased, and attendance of the new service is above the critical mass, go with it! At the same time continue evaluating why your original target audience is not responding in a manner you had anticipated. What you learn will help when you begin planning your next new service.

Evaluating Relevance

One of the best ways to evaluate whether the message and style of your service is on target is to get feedback—from spies. Or a more acceptable term might be "outside observers." Have several church members ask friends to visit your new service as anonymous observers. The purpose is to get candid feedback on the service from newcomers and solicit suggestions about how to make the service better. Here's why this idea is well worth the effort:

1. No one who is involved in the planning and presentation of the new service can tell how the service truly comes across to the visitor. That perspective can only come from a visitor. But most visitors who attend the service do not expect to be grilled afterward. A person specifically invited to attend a service as an observer will be prepared to share his or her thoughts and will provide a unique and valuable perspective.
2. Some church members who might not otherwise be comfortable inviting a friend to the service will do so if the invitation is to be an observer and provide feedback.
3. Who knows? The visitors might actually discover that the service is a positive experience and return next week!

Develop a short questionnaire that the member can give to the friend to evaluate the visit. (See appendix E.) Following the service the member should meet with the friend to evaluate the experience and make additional notes. Distribute copies of the visitor's completed evaluation to the appropriate people.

Evaluating Performance

Part of an effective worship service is performance. When you plan the order of service, prepare the sermon, test the sound and lights, or arrange the platform, you are preparing for a performance. This fact does not trivialize or illegitimatize the holiness of the service. It simply states that when you have leaders in the front of the sanctuary and observers in the pews, you have a performance. Even the service in a small country church is a performance.

A considerable amount of the difference between large or growing churches and small or declining churches is simply the quality of the performance. Consequently, an important part of evaluating your new service is to ask, How was the performance?

The best way to answer this is to videotape your service. Ask a member to set up a tripod and camcorder with a sound jack into the PA system. Keep the zoom on medium close-ups of platform personnel (versus a static long-shot). Then, during the following week, sit down with the worship coordinator and review the tape in detail. Imagine you are sitting in the pew participating in the experience.

When you evaluate the service, look for whether the message came through. Did the people leave with the message you intended? Next evaluate individual aspects of the service, including the opening, each segment, and the pace and transitions of the service. Was the sound and lighting quality as high as possible? Was audience involvement appropriate? Focus on changes that can be made in coming weeks to improve the performance.

Pastors may wish to review the sermon in particular. "While it requires considerable courage and a strong desire for self-improvement, watching oneself delivering a sermon on videotape can be both a humbling and enlightening experience."[4]

Six Months' Evaluation

Approximately six months after the first new service, church leaders should meet to evaluate the service and decide on its long-term disposition. At that time the most powerful argument in favor of continuing the new service will be an overall increase in the number of people experiencing the church's ministry. Conversely, if there is no increase in the number of people who have begun attending a service, it is reasonable to ask whether the dedication of time, money, people, and energy is worth the effort.

While 80 percent of the churches that begin a new service experience an increase in total attendance, approximately 20 percent find that the new service has simply divided their present con-

211

gregation. If, after a four- to six-month experimental period, your combined attendance has not grown beyond the attendance prior to starting the new service, your options are: (1) drop the new service; (2) redesign the new service; (3) keep the new service. None of these options are palatable:

Option 1: Dropping the service will be widely interpreted as failure and will create a general sense of discouragement within the church, particularly among those who tried to make it a success. To make matters worse, many of the active proponents of the new service will leave to attend other churches.

Option 2: Redesigning the service assumes that the low attendance was due to the style of the service. While this may be true, it is likely there were other reasons. An accurate post-mortem of a new service is difficult since there are so many possible reasons or combinations of reasons for failure. The redesign option also assumes that people will begin attending once the ingredients have been rearranged. This is seldom the case. Enough people will have tried the service or heard about it and decided not to attend that you no longer have a large prospect pool from which to draw your critical mass.

Option 3: Nor is the third option of keeping the service as it is a desirable prospect. The longer a new service continues in a nongrowth mode, the more difficult it is to see growth begin. Two weak services is better than one weak service, and there is no evidence that combining two weak services results in one healthy service. But to see a service poorly attended week after week will be discouraging to all involved and contribute to declining morale and corporate self-esteem. To say nothing of the extra energy such a service requires of staff and volunteers.

All of which is another reason to put your very best effort and people into making the new service successful the first time.

212

Figure 39

Attendance Growth of Reading First Presbyterian Church

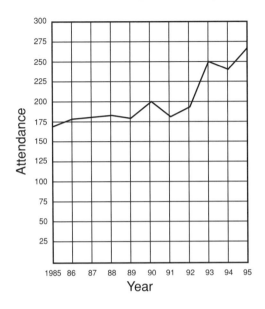

Year

On the positive side, if your experience is similar to the 80 per-cent of churches that begin a new service, your graph of total attendance will look something like that of First Presbyterian Church (Reading, Pa.) after it added a new service in 1993 (see fig. 39).

Using the Evaluation as an Ally

Keep your ear out for personal stories resulting from your new service. Are there people who have begun attending after years outside the church? Are there marriages that have been resur-rected because of the new service? Are there children of long-term members who have begun attending? Use these life stories, appro-priately, to reinforce the "rightness" of the church's decision to add a new service. In newsletters, personal conversation, and

213

reports to church leadership, changed lives will be (or at least should be) the eventual criterion used to decide whether the new service should be kept or killed.

When the new service is helping your church reach its mission and touch people's lives, it will be difficult for Late Adopters to make a case for returning to the status quo. Keep a written file of stories, comments, testimonies, and experiences that support the value of the new service. Use them frequently during the first three to six months or until the decision has been made on the long-term disposition of the new service.

10

Getting People
to Come Back

∽

What percentage of people who first visit the worship service of a growing church become regular attenders in the following year? Fifty percent? Seventy-five percent? Ninety percent?

The answer might surprise you. Most growing churches keep only 21 percent of their first-time visitors—two out of ten.

The difference with those that are not growing might also surprise you. In churches in which the worship attendance is plateauing or declining, first-time visitor retention rate is just under one in ten (9 percent). But the difference between growing churches and nongrowing churches—two of ten versus one of ten—is enough to make the difference between overall growth or decline.[1]

If you average only two of every ten visitors to your new service becoming active, your attendance will grow. The key to making this growth equation work involves two variables: (1) sufficient number of first-time visitors attending, and (2) 20 percent or more of those visitors returning. In chapter 8 we looked at the first issue—how to see enough visitors initially attend. Now let's consider how to see sufficient numbers return.

Before we begin, it is necessary to state one important assumption: *Your service is worth coming back for.* The best follow-up strategies in the world will be useless if the message is irrelevant, the music inappropriate, and the experience unpleasant. But if you have done your homework, and if the evaluation of the new service is positive, there are ways to increase the number of visitors who return.

What Do You Call Them?

First I'd like to recommend that you don't call your visitors *visitors*. I define visitor as "a person who resides temporarily; one who goes or comes to inspect; one who makes a short stay at a place for a particular purpose."

Rather, refer to your newcomers as guests. Introduce this term into the vocabulary of your church leaders as they discuss and describe those who are attending for the first (and second and third) time. A guest is defined as "a person welcomed into one's house; a person to whom hospitality is extended; a person held in honor who is due special courtesies."

It is surprising how our language affects our perception of others, which in turn affects our behavior toward them. Calling newcomers guests rather than visitors is a first step toward extending to them the honor and importance they deserve.

Who Greets Your Guests?

Most churches that welcome new attenders station greeters near the front door of the church or sanctuary entrance. A nice gesture, but one that does not contribute much to seeing guests return.

A greeter is "one who meets or extends welcome in a specified manner; one who gives a formal salutation at a meeting."

Let me suggest that you begin using a new term, which implies an entirely different role and relationship: host. I define the term as "one who receives or entertains socially; one who opens his or her home for a special event; one who takes particular care and concern that guests are well accommodated."

Research indicates the most important question guests are asking during their first visit is: Is this a friendly church? And the primary way they determine the answer is through the number of people who initiate a conversation with them.

First impressions begin the moment your guests drive into your parking lot. It's an important moment because you'll never have a second chance for a good first impression. As a result, I encourage churches to deploy "parking hosts" in areas where people will be getting out of their cars to attend your service. This includes porticos where passengers are dropped off, street parking areas, public parking, church parking lots. On rainy days, parking hosts should have umbrellas to distribute and escort those who need help. Parking hosts should be well acquainted with Sunday school classrooms, the nursery, restrooms, and general directions. A printed map of the church campus should be given to any newcomer who seems to need one.

Once your guests are inside the building, another group should be ready to extend the welcome mat—"foyer hosts." These people take overcoats or umbrellas and hang them up for guests. They may escort a child to a classroom or a mother to the nursery. They may even sit with guests during the service if it seems appropriate. Obviously, more than just several foyer hosts will be necessary to effectively welcome all guests.

In the sanctuary, your guests will be served by "service hosts." Faith Community Church (Covina, Calif.) has developed a creative and effective way to help newcomers feel welcomed. Two service hosts are designated for each zone of pews and are stationed at every fourth row on the end of the row (see fig. 40). The service hosts take their positions in the sanctuary ten to fifteen minutes prior to the service.

The task of the service hosts is to greet everyone who sits in their zone. They welcome guests, engage them in conversation, and introduce them to others sitting near them. Immediately following the service, they are the first ones to go to the guests, thank them for coming, and encourage them to come back.

These service hosts can also be responsible for the offering in their zone. Each team needs only two offering plates to handle four rows. With this arrangement an offering can take less than thirty seconds.

Figure 40

Service Host Zones and Responsibility

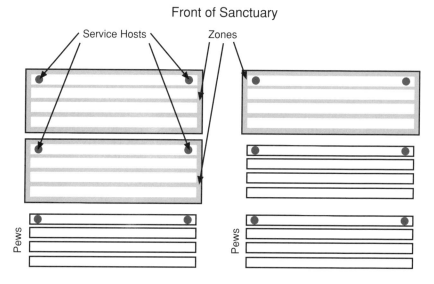

After the Service

The most common reason visitors give for returning to a church is "the friendliness of the people."[2] However, interviews I have conducted with guests indicate there is one ten-minute window during the overall visit in which newcomers are most (or least) impressed with the church's "friendliness." That window is the ten minutes following the conclusion of the service. During this relatively brief time, more than at any other time, newcomers are assessing whether the people at this church are genuinely friendly or if it is just an act. Up until the service concludes, it is easy for newcomers to follow the "rules" and get lost in the crowd. But once the final prayer is said, all rules are off. If people in the church seem friendly and caring immediately after the service, research tells us it makes a significant impression on newcomers, particularly if they have come alone.

While the ten minutes following the service is the most important time for making guests feel welcome, the coffee time is the second most important. So let's talk coffee. This hallowed moment in the Sunday morning schedule can be one of the most effective—or one of the most destructive—ways to extend a welcome to newcomers.

If guests come to the service alone, the chances are good that they will not even make it to the coffee table on their own; it's simply too socially threatening. A visiting couple may go together, but they will not stay long unless someone engages them in conversation.

Consequently, I suggest you have a fourth set of hosts following your new service—"coffee hosts." Coffee hosts stay in the coffee-and-cookies area (you should have no trouble finding volunteers) and are constantly on the lookout for newcomers standing alone. Their task is to engage these people in conversation and not leave them alone until they have introduced the guests to someone else in the coffee area.

A coffee area where guests are ignored is worse than no coffee area at all. If guests visit your coffee area but no one seems to notice their existence, you may as well hand them a three-by-five card that reads, "Do you want into this church? Well, plan on working very hard. Because it won't be easy." Most will read your "card," leave, and not return.

Having an intentional plan for welcoming guests does not mean your welcome is artificial. It means you care enough about extending a welcome to newcomers that you have a plan to see it happen. An effective welcome is one of your best ways to assure you'll make a good first impression with guests who visit your new service. It also allows a larger number of members to be involved in welcoming newcomers. And as these members perform their duty on the days they are assigned as hosts, they will be increasingly friendly with guests when they are "off duty." And most important, your newcomers will feel welcomed and be far more likely to return.

What Newcomers Are Looking For

Bob Bast, in his research for the popular book *Attracting New Members*,[3] found that people are looking for certain things in a service. When newcomers find many or all of those ingredients, they are inclined to return. What are people looking for when they visit a church?

1. *The friendliness and warmth of the church.* A study by the United Methodist Church found that "when both unchurched and churched people are asked what they look for in a church, all agree on one factor—they are looking for a church in which they feel at home, where the people are friendly, and where there is a warm and comfortable atmosphere."[4]

2. *The character of the worship service.* People want to experience the presence of God. They are looking for clarity and guidance to know what is right, and the power to do what is right. People also need affirmation of the reality and depth of God's love. And they want to leave uplifted, not beat down; they want to be strengthened and equipped for life.

3. *A place for children.* Recent studies show that visitors perceive the needs of their children as a major factor in their decision to find a church. Churches that provide opportunities for children will be effective in attracting people.

4. *The adult program.* One way to attract unchurched adults is to offer activities in which they can participate. Athletic events, classes, musical and fitness groups, and social gatherings can be designed to include unchurched people.

5. *The church building.* Facilities don't cause a church to grow, but they can prevent it. Four key questions are: Is the church visible? Is the church accessible? What is the condition of your property? Do you have adequate space? Newcomers are looking for modern and well-kept facilities.

Follow-Up

Discussing follow-up is rather pointless if you don't have a way of obtaining the names and addresses of your guests. Here is a suggested monologue for the pastor or worship leader to give in your new service as you welcome guests:

Good morning, my name is Pastor _____. On behalf of the family here at _____, I would like to welcome you this morning. If you're a visitor with us today, we want you to know that you are our guest and that it's our privilege to have you here. And we want you to know that you're welcome to come back.

If you're here for the first time, we know that you probably have more questions than answers. To help answer some of your questions, we've prepared a special packet of information just for you. If you'll identify yourself to the closest host [here is another role your service hosts can fill], we will give you this packet.

Inside this packet you'll find a brochure that tells you a little about our church, and a welcome letter from me telling you what we're about and how glad we are that you are with us. You'll also find a guest registration card and a pencil. But before I ask you to fill that out, I just want to give you the assurance that no one from this church will show up on your doorstep unannounced. What we would like to do is put you on our mailing list so you can get further information about our church. And a friendly layperson from our church will be giving you a phone call in the next day or so to answer any questions and see if there is any way we can be of further assistance to you.

The number one fear that unchurched people have in filling out a registration card is that they are going to get an unannounced visit. Practice the principle of disclosure with your guests, being forthright about what will be done with the information. And then do what you say. You'll find that guests are far more willing to share their lives with you.

Following up on your guests is not necessary to grow a new service or a church. In fact, many megachurches don't even follow up guests with a letter, let alone a phone call. But if they were to implement an effective follow-up strategy, my experience indicates they would increase their guest return rate by 20 to 25 percent. And so will you. For your new service in particular, that increase in the number of visitors who return is well worth the effort.

One reason that it is worthwhile to put energy into guest follow-up is that every additional person in attendance brings you closer to the critical mass for your new service—that threshold at which the new service can begin to grow by its own momentum. As we mentioned, the sooner you reach your critical mass, the more certain and more rapid will be your growth beyond that point. Everything you can do to put people in the pews during the first critical months of your new service will return itself tenfold.

However, a more important reason to follow up with guests is that by so doing, you are being a good steward of the people God has brought into your sphere of influence. The parable of the lost sheep (Luke 15:3–7) suggests that God places great value on each individual who comes into the flock. And if only one sheep wanders away, the good shepherd sets off to look for it. Of course, not all guests will become members. But you can expect a measurable increase in your guest return rate with a strategy that integrates effective follow-up principles.

The Results of Follow-Up

The Johari window in figure 41 identifies four scenarios relating the quality of your service to the quality of your follow-up. Your own situation will fit into one of the four categories.

Your service quality (be it good or poor) and your follow-up (good or poor) have a measurable effect on guest return rates. Based on my research and experience with churches adding a new service, the formulas in figure 42 illustrate the effect of service quality and guest follow-up on attendance. *A* represents the average attendance after the first month. The factor following *A* represents the effect of each scenario on your attendance six months later.

For example, suppose you began with an average attendance of 75 people in your new service after the first month. If you have a good service but poor follow-up (represented in the top left box), you could expect to see your average attendance increase to approximately 94 people by the end of the sixth month (75 x 1.25). If,

222

Figure 41

Service Quality and Follow-Up Quality Options

Good Service Poor Follow-Up	Good Service Good Follow-Up
Poor Service Poor Follow-Up	Poor Service Good Follow-Up

Figure 42

Effect of Follow-Up on Attendance Six Months Later

Good Service Poor Follow-Up **(A) x 1.25**	Good Service Good Follow-Up **(A) x 1.50**
Poor Service Poor Follow-Up **(A) x .25**	Poor Service Good Follow-Up **(A) x .50**

however, you have a good service and a good follow-up strategy, total attendance should be close to 112 people (75 x 1.50).

If the quality of the service is poor (that is, guests conclude that the benefit is not worth the cost), but you have a good follow-up strategy, you could expect the average attendance to drop to 37 or 38 people within six months (75 x .50). If both the service and

223

the follow-up are poor, total attendance will drop to 19 or 20 people (75 x .25) in six months.

Effective Follow-Up

We have already spent considerable time in this book on the first variable—a quality service. Let's look for a moment at some guidelines for effective follow-up. These five simple but important principles will help you increase the number of newcomers who eventually become regular attenders at your new service. The more of these principles you practice, the more guests will return.

Time Principle

Contact guests within forty-eight hours of their visit. The first two days provide your best window for a follow-up contact with guests. The longer you wait beyond the first two days, the fewer people will return the following week. Figure 43 illustrates newcomer return rates based on when the follow-up contact was made.

The follow-up contact need not (and increasingly, these days, should not) be an unannounced visit to the home. In most communities, a stranger knocking at the front door is an anxiety-provoking event. The risk of offending your recent guest with an unannounced visit is far greater than any benefit of having face-to-face contact. The medium of choice is the telephone. It is nearly as personal, less intimidating (for both caller and callee), and more efficient.

The caller (ideally the service host) should introduce himself or herself and explain that he or she called to simply thank the person for attending and answer any questions about the church. If there are no questions, the caller should briefly share the theme of next week's service and invite the guest to return. If the service host makes the call, the guest should be invited to sit in the same area the following Sunday to continue the relationship. The caller might comment on some particularly outstanding part of the church's ministry if it relates to the guest's interest.

224

Figure 43

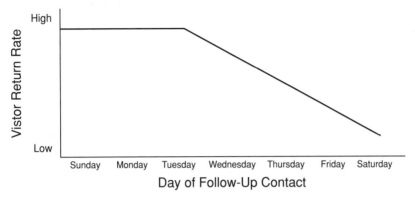

Visitor Return Rate Based on Follow-Up Contact Day

Purpose Principle

The goal of the follow-up contact is to see guests return. Research helps clarify the importance of this principle. We mentioned earlier that in the average (albeit nongrowing) church, 10 to 12 percent of first-time guests become active in the church within one year. (In growing churches, remember, approximately 20 percent of first-time guests become active.) However, there is an additional insight, perhaps even more important, with respect to seeing guests return: The more often a person visits, the more likely he or she is to remain. Consider the following:[5]

Guest Retention Rate*

	Nongrowing Churches (under 5%/yr.)	Growing Churches (over 5%/yr.)
First-time guest	9%	21%
Second-time guest	17%	38%
Third-time guest	36%	57%

* "Guest retention rate" is the percentage of people who visit a church and are still regularly attending the same church one year following that visit.

225

This information shouts loud and clear that the chance of a guest becoming a regular attender essentially doubles every time he or she returns. A person who attends your new service two times over a period of several months is twice as likely to be a regular attender as a person who visits only once. And a person who attends three times in a short period of time is more likely to be active than even a second-time guest.

Unfortunately, many churches make the mistake of trying to make evangelistic calls instead of follow-up calls. These churches mistakenly assume that once someone visits their service, the church has permission to intrude into their lives with an uninvited call to give unsolicited answers to unasked questions. Such an approach has been shown to be counterproductive for effective disciple-making.[6] The goal of your follow-up contact should be nothing more, and nothing less, than to see guests return the following week.

Personnel Principle

Laity should make the follow-up contacts. The guest return-rate to your new service will double when a layperson makes the follow-up contact. That's the positive way to phrase it. An equally true statement, though somewhat more humbling for many clergy, is that when the pastor makes the call, the return rate drops by half.[7]

Why would this be true? Why would more guests return when invited by a layperson than by a church staff member? A pastor once answered this question in one of my seminars by joking, "Preachers are paid to be good; laypeople are good for nothing!" In a sense, he is right. When newcomers are contacted by the pastor, they know that the pastor is being paid and that part of the job is to make such calls.

In contrast, when a guest is contacted by a layperson, the experience is perceived by the newcomer as considerably more "believable." In fact, a lay member bragging about the pastor to a church guest is one of the best ways to raise the stature of the pastor in the eyes of the newcomer. Of course, the opposite kinds of comments about a pastor are given equal validity. (Pastors: Choose your callers carefully!)

How can you find such a large number of laypeople willing to serve as either hosts or follow-up callers? The secret is to ask for help infrequently.

Most churches request members to serve lengthy terms as greeters or phone callers. A better approach is to ask every member to serve as a host or caller only several times a year. Members can select the dates they would like to host or call, even trade them with other members if a conflict arises. The process involves many members and is a minimal duty to expect from anyone who joins the church.

Entry Path Principle

Create opportunities for newcomers to get involved. Here are two similar but different terms that have come out of the church growth movement: *entry event* and *entry path*. An entry event is a high-visibility activity sponsored by the church for the purpose of inviting and attracting newcomers. Your new service is an example of a creative entry event. A good church outreach strategy will include a variety of entry events (community festivals, parenting seminars, Christmas cantata, vacation Bible school, pancake breakfast, divorce recovery seminar, health fair).

But entry events do not by themselves grow churches. Just check your recent additions to the membership roll as a result of your last three VBSs or Christmas cantatas. Entry events introduce the church to new people, but if that's all the church offers for newcomers, they generally remain observers.

You also need entry paths. These are small groups, special classes, or ongoing activities in which people can feel like participants, not just observers. It is here they begin feeling comfortable in church-sponsored activities and start building relationships with others in the church. It is in the entry path experiences that people become assimilated into active church fellowship.

Research indicates that 75 to 90 percent of all people who join a church do so because of a friend or relative already in the church.[8] The more friends that unchurched people make in your church, the more comfortable they will be and the more likely they will want to continue. Entry events are the doors into your church; entry paths are the rooms where people get acquainted.

Effective entry paths into your church will follow up on the research of your target audience by providing appropriate opportunities for people to get involved in areas of personal interest or need. If your new service focuses on Baby Boomers, for example, it is appropriate to offer classes or groups of interest to Baby Boomers. If your service is geared toward seekers, a Bible study from a nonbeliever's perspective would be a good entry path.

Infrastructure Principle

The more small groups you provide, the more newcomers will get involved. Small groups are the best entry path you can create for newcomers to become active, responsible members. They supplement a person's spiritual growth, as well as build the relationships that are the key to assimilation. But to effectively assimilate newcomers, most churches need more small groups than they have at present. Do you have enough? Here are three ratios to help you find out:[9]

Small-group ratio—7:100. For every one hundred active members, a church should have seven small, face-to-face groups. This ratio provides enough groups so that everyone who wants to be involved can be.

Newcomer-involvement ratio—8:10. Eighty percent of all new members should be involved in a small group within six months. Newcomers are more willing to join a group than are long-term members. And it is important that they do to nurture and grow new relationships in the church.

New-group ratio—1:5. Twenty percent of the groups in your church should have been started within the last two years. Nine of every ten groups in your church will lose their ability to incorporate new people after two years of existence. Because of this "saturation point" phenomena, it is essen-

228

tial to regularly start new groups so newcomers can get involved.

The scope of this book does not allow for an in-depth discussion on how, why, when, and where to start small groups. I would encourage you to explore the variety of helpful books available on this topic. One of my favorites is *How to Start and Grow Small Groups* by Jeanne Hipp.[10]

In Conclusion

The goal of all your efforts of research, planning, promotion, and conducting a new service is to reach new people with the good news of Christ's love. Being good stewards of those new men, women, and children that God has brought into your life demands the same caring and intentional priority that Jesus himself gave to those people who came into his path.

Epilogue

I hope you have seen some new possibilities of outreach and growth for your church. It has been my privilege to share in the joy of pastors and churches who have discovered that they really can be an instrument of outreach into their community and of change in the lives of people through a new service.

Many church leaders—perhaps you among them—have read the "success" stories or attended the seminars of churches that seem to have figured it all out. How easy it seems for them, and how difficult for us.

I won't be so presumptuous as to suggest that a new service in your church is the simple solution to all your problems. But I can tell you with utmost certainty that there is opportunity in your church for exciting new growth and vitality. As long as there are unreached people groups in your community, there is an opportunity for God's love to be shared with them. For many of these people, it may well be through a new service.

Whenever I start feeling there is little chance for me to ever realize such far-fetched dreams, I like to recall a story I discovered a few years ago. It's a true story that took place high in the Rocky Mountains over one hundred years ago. Let me share it with you as an encouragement to see possibilities of new growth in your church, quite possibly through a new service in the near future.

"Gold! Gold!" were the shouts echoing through the hills near the town of Leadville, Colorado, in 1862. The country was in the midst of the gold rush, and men by the thousands were searching for fortunes in the bottom of their panning tins.

The nearby California Gulch (named after the gold dreams of the Forty-niners out West) attracted many of the newcomers to Leadville because of its rich potential and strategic placement. But it quickly earned a nasty reputation among the prospectors. "It's that black sand!" they complained. "It gums up the riffles in the sluice boxes. It fills panning holes we dug the day before. It stains and ruins clothes." The black sand seemed to cover every gold nugget with grime and grit and make a mockery of any attempt to find one's fortune. While prospectors came to Leadville in great numbers, they soon left discouraged, cursing the black sand and moving on in search of easier streams to riches. Sixteen years later the ruins of Leadville told of a boomtown gone bust. Only the remnants of abandoned cabins and sluice boxes remained.

To the abandoned mines and sluice boxes of the California Gulch came two mining men, William H. Stevens and Alvinus B. Wood. Convinced there was still gold beneath the surface, they began buying up old claims. Initial gold finds heightened their expectations. But soon they too encountered the problems of the earlier prospectors. The black sand hampered progress until it appeared the entire project would fall victim to the wretched grit.

One day Stevens decided to send a sample of "that black stuff" to the East Coast for analysis. To their surprise, the men found that the black sand was lead carbonate—loaded with silver!

Stevens and Wood staked lode claims throughout the California Gulch and opened the Rock Mine, the first silver-producing mine in the district. They became fabulously rich in a matter of years!

The black sand that miners and prospectors had cursed as an abominable intrusion in the pursuit of their golden dreams contained wealth that would have made them rich beyond their wildest imaginations. The sandy California Gulch yielded a pittance in gold but a fortune in silver.

Around your church, at this very moment, are opportunities to reach people hidden in the "black sand." They are people who represent great value to God. They are needy. They are receptive. They are waiting to be found. While your present worship service may not be the tool to mine this treasure, a new service designed to reach them with God's love could help you experience wonderful new discoveries of ministry and growth. What now appears to be a frustrating problem of how to reach new people could lead to riches in ministry and growth beyond your wildest imagination!

God bless you as you discover the exciting new opportunities available to you.

Appendix A

Prayer Group Agenda

The following are suggestions for leading a group of people in exploring God's will for a new service in the church.

Prayer

The first and foremost purpose of the group is prayer. Of the time spent together, at least half should be spent in prayer. Ask God for understanding and wisdom in considering the possibility of a new service. Pray that your lack of faith would not inhibit God's power to move in your church. And encourage each person in attendance to open his or her heart and mind to what God wants to do to reach people in your community.

Bible Study

A brief study from a relevant Bible passage will add to the insight and prayer of the group.

A fascinating study is about the New Testament church wrestling with the culture barrier. The first-century Jewish Christians found it difficult to accept Gentile believers because of cultural differences that they found ungodly and at times offensive. Acts 10 tells about a Gentile named Cornelius. It was to his house that the apostle Peter was called by a vision. God sent Peter, a culturally entrenched Jewish fisherman, to this Gentile's house to bring the message of the Good News.

As a result, Cornelius and his household became believers. But they didn't reject their Gentile culture when they accepted a faith in Christ. Cornelius was firm in his commitment but comfortable in his culture. God used one of the most Jewish of disciples to open the door for a household of Gentiles to come to faith without coming into the Jewish culture or adopting the Jewish paradigm.

Later, Acts 15 records how other Jewish believers who were not comfortable with the idea that Gentiles should be sought after as new converts. Some contended that to be a "true" follower of Christ one must become part of the Jewish culture; that is, learn to see the world from a Jewish perspective and adopt the Jewish paradigm. Others disagreed. The council of Jerusalem met in an effort to settle this disagreement among the Jewish believers.

You can almost hear the conversation: "If we let those people in, who knows what will happen? The church will change; we'll all be compromised. The gospel must remain pure!"

It must have been a serious, heart-wrenching struggle for many of those early believers. After all, their understanding of the gospel was solely from their Jewish perspective. What would the gospel look like expressed in a Gentile world? Could it even remain the gospel? And could they risk that possibility?

In the end, the council determined it was possible for Gentiles to be "full" believers and still function within the Gentile culture. The early church came to realize that cultural differences are not moral differences or theological differences. Nor do they prohibit those of another culture from coming to life-changing faith in Jesus Christ. No one individual worldview—no one paradigm of culture—is divine. And because of that historic decision, the gospel spread from Jewish Jerusalem to "the ends of the earth."

Discussion Questions

1. Would the gospel have likely been endorsed by the Gentiles if the Jewish Christians had demanded that they also practice the Jewish rituals?
2. Are there parallels between the first-century church's struggles and situations of today?
3. Do we sometimes think people must become part of "our culture" when they become Christians?

Sharing and Learning

Part of the goal for the prayer group should be an increased understanding of your own church's growth dynamics related to a new service.

Charts and graphs based on your church's statistics will help the group focus on the needs and opportunities you are facing. Before the first meeting, research, graph, and duplicate information about

- church membership for the past ten years.
- worship attendance for the past ten years.
- population growth within fifteen minutes' travel of your church.

If available, bring the following information to the meeting:

- Percentage of visitors compared with total attendance during the past five years. (Growing churches average 4 to 5 percent of their total morning worship attendance as first- or second-time visitors. This seems to be the number necessary to both make up for backdoor losses and then to grow beyond that point. If your church has less than 4 percent of your total attendance as visitors, growth will not likely occur. A new service is one excellent way to increase the "visitor flow.")

237

- Percentage of visitors who joined your church within a year of their first visit. (Growing churches average between 18 to 20 percent of first-time visitors who eventually join. Plateaued churches average 10 to 12 percent.)

Personal Illustrations

Statistics and charts are important, but the real business of the church is people. At each meeting of your prayer group, share at least one story of a person who has recently experienced personal and/or spiritual growth through the ministry of the church. Include stories of several relatively new members if possible. Point out to those in the group that their church is God's ambassador on earth. Also, some of your church members probably have friends or family who are not attending church or are attending another church because your existing service does not meet their needs. If this situation would shed light on the idea of a new service to reach a new target group—including these friends or family—share these situations as well.

These are tangible illustrations of what the church is called to do—help others experience the joy and healing of God's love. Explain that the goal of your church should be to allow as many hurting people as possible to experience that love. Note that a new service has the potential to significantly increase the number of people who are touched by the ministry of your church.

Appendix B

Questions and Answers
about a New Service

The following is a copy of a bulletin insert developed and distributed by the First Church of the Nazarene (Pasadena, Calif.) as a means of presenting to members answers to questions about their upcoming new service.

Our congregation was recently asked to respond to a questionnaire regarding two different Sunday morning worship options. The questionnaire raised some good questions that needed a response for the benefit of the entire congregation. The following are those questions and answers.

Question: Why are two worship service options being studied?

Answer: Our vision statement states that we intend for ministry to be offered with "a diversity of options." This means any options offered take into consideration the needs of our church family and those of our local community.

In the previous questionnaire, the terms *contemporary* and *traditional* were used. Your pastors have realized that these terms spoke to style more than to motive. The need for a seeker-targeted worship service is based on an attempt to reach people in our community who have little or no church experience. Several of the comments on the questionnaire made it obvious that some in our congregation saw the earlier service as an opportunity to invite friends who probably would not immediately be comfortable in the traditional worship service.

Since the average age of the people living within a ten-mile radius of the church is thirty-four, the style of the service would have an appeal to a younger generation without church experience. Those who come to know the Lord for the first time as adults and come to our present worship and Sunday school experiences often feel lost with no preparation for all that they are experiencing. Both experience and research indicate that seeker-sensitive worship would allow us to have a significant impact on local people not now a part of our church fellowship nor of another church fellowship. Churches in the United States which have offered a seeker-sensitive worship experience have been far more successful in bringing new believers to the Lord than churches which have not done so.

Question: Can you describe what a seeker-sensitive worship service would be like?

Answer: Actually the seeker-sensitive worship service and traditional worship service have similar components but vary in style. While the biblical text and sermon would deal with the same subject in both services, there would be different approaches.

Because experience is vital, we have scheduled two seeker-sensitive worship services on May 16 and June 27 at the 10:45 A.M. time as we worship together. [Author's note: Staff members decided later to change their approach and offer a choice of service styles for those who did not wish to attend the contemporary service.]

Question: If these two worship services are scheduled on a weekly basis for the future, how would this affect our Sunday school classes?

Answer: After we experience the new style of worship in May and June, Sunday school classes will have a discussion among their membership concerning preferences for the earlier or later worship service. While Sunday school classes will be offered during both the first and second worship experiences, no Sunday school class will be asked to change from the first hour that they now experience. However, if a majority of class members decide that they would like their class to change, we would work with them on making that shift. This will be the choice of the class members.

After all of the classes respond with their intentions, we would then determine what other classes need to be added during the first and second hours. Classes for all age groups would be offered during each of the hours. Since the seeker-sensitive worship service will be during the first hour, some classes designed to be more seeker sensitive would be scheduled during the second hour. This will include a "track" to introduce guests to the basic fundamentals of faith, opportunities to accept Christ, and knowledge about our beliefs. The adult Sunday school teachers are also working concurrently on a coordinated curriculum to enhance the biblical literacy of everyone in our church fellowship.

Since we're using every space available for our Sunday morning classes now, being able to add classes during two different hours would be a benefit. New opportunities this year have significantly increased the number of people involved in classes.

Question: Will this put additional pressure on children's ministries in attempting to recruit children's workers?

Answer: We believe quite the contrary. The children's pastors indicate that since they do programming both hours for children now, this will not be substantially different. In addition, two worship options will give every worker the option to be in a worship service on a Sunday morning. This is not now the case, since many workers are with children during the only worship experience. We believe many others would take the opportunity to work with the children if they knew it meant they could be in a worship experience during the other hour.

Question: Doesn't this put too much pressure on Pastor Green in preparing for two worship services?

Answer: Pastor Green looks forward to the possibility of reaching more people with the gospel, discipling them into a relationship with Christ, and integrating them into our church fellowship. When he came here a year ago as our pastor, he fully anticipated that we would be moving to multiple worship options because of all the above stated reasons. His previous church had

241

moved to two services prior to his move here, and they still continue both of those worship options today.

Question: Do two worship options fragment the church family?

Answer: The best analogy for the church family and for what we believe theologically in terms of church growth is that we are like a cell that continues to divide and multiply. As we grow larger, "a diversity of options" allows us to be most effective in the lives of the people we reach. The facility that we now occupy was built so we could continue to grow when it was no longer possible to park cars and meet needs adequately at the previous facility. As discussions for our church facility were taking place two decades ago, there were discussions about the day when multiple worship services would be necessary on this campus.

Also, there are continuing issues being addressed regarding parking and needs associated with increased numbers of people coming to this campus on a Sunday morning. We believe our campus has unlimited possibilities that we have only begun to use in reaching people for Christ.

Question: What is the impact of this on the church family, since many people will be in different worship services?

Answer: We are looking at specific ways that allow us to relate as church family outside of worship. There would still be a family sense in worship even with two distinct services. Since options will be available for Sunday school and worship, families would need to discuss how the members of the family would worship and go to classes. One family responded that their college-age son would never come to a worship service as we now have it; however, they believe he would come to an earlier seeker-sensitive worship service, and they would attend that service with him just for the joy of having him come and being together.

Question: When would we begin two services?

Answer: When all issues have been discussed in our open dialogue and understanding seems clear, we would move ahead together. We believe that the opportunities to experience the seeker-sensitive worship service and the traditional worship service in May and June will help that to happen. Task forces are also working on the issues of parking, technical services, hospitality staffing, and so on. Based on these issues and on the experiences we have together in worship, we could project a timetable for beginning the two worship experiences.

Research indicates that while churches are growing in America today (and some of them to sizes previously unseen), the overall number of people coming to know the Lord and involved in church has been decreasing in the United States. Statistics also reveal that most churches of four hundred or more are simply reshuffling and reprocessing the saints from other churches as they add to their numbers. We are committed to something different— reaching those with little or no church experience whom few are touching today.

Appendix C

Conducting Successful
Focus Groups

Here are some guidelines for conducting research on your target audience using focus groups. This is an excellent means of learning about attitudes, needs, issues, and opinions that will help in planning a relevant new service.

There are a number of activities involved in conducting successful focus groups. Here are the major areas to which one or more persons should be assigned.

Finding a Location

The ideal location is a neutral site that has been specifically designed to conduct focus groups. That is, the room is relatively small, it has a two-way mirror for observation, and it has a microphone and speaker so that the conversation can be monitored in the observation room. Such locations may often be found in universities, counseling centers, and business complexes.

If an ideal room cannot be located, the second choice would be in a neutral location with a secluded room, such as a restaurant, motel, school, or office. The disadvantage of not having a room with a two-way mirror is that it is more difficult for observers to be present and benefit from the comments shared.

Recruiting Participants

The ideal number for a focus group is eight to twelve. Less than eight people tends to cast doubt on the validity of the information obtained. More than twelve makes the focus group difficult to manage and limits the interaction between participants.

People invited to participate in the focus group should be representative of your target audience. The best way to invite people to participate is a telephone call or personal invitation. Since it is likely that only one of every three people will be able to participate, it is best to make a list of somewhere between twenty-five and thirty-five people to contact for each group.

People are most likely to accept an invitation to participate in a focus group if they are invited by a person they know who is a member of the church. Ask church members to explain to the people they are inviting that the church is researching the community and the needs to which the church might respond. Most people (members and nonmembers) do not find such an invitation to be inappropriate or difficult to accept.

A second option is to send a letter to selected people in this target group, asking for their participation. The letter should include a postage-paid response card. It is not uncommon in business-oriented focus groups for participants to be reimbursed fifteen to twenty-five dollars for their time. You should decide if you feel this is appropriate.

Leading the Focus Group

Focus groups are best led by a person other than the pastor. The leader is responsible for preparing the questions and directing the discussion. The focus group should last approximately fifty minutes. The goal is to create an environment in which group members feel free to share their feelings and attitudes about the topics discussed. A series of questions is used by the focus group leader to guide the discussion; however, the direction of the discussion frequently reflects the issues raised during the actual session.

In a sense, the focus group is similar to a group therapy session. That is, the purpose of the time together is to find out how group members feel about a particular issue. There are no right or wrong answers. When a comment is made, it may be followed up by the focus group leader, or clarification may be requested, or other members in the group may be asked to respond to the comment. Therefore the focus group leader should be sensitive to group interaction and be able to bring out the thoughts and feelings of people on various topics.

Questions that might serve as a guide for a focus group meeting are suggested later in this appendix. These questions may be modified to fit your particular target group and situation.

Summarizing the Information

Immediately following the focus group, the leader and observers from the church should meet and evaluate the session. (Observers may wish to make notes throughout the session as well as during the discussion afterward.) Try to develop some key generalizations from the session, particularly related to the service in the church.

Providing Refreshments

Participants in the focus groups should be treated as guests. They will probably arrive prior to the starting time, so refreshments (coffee, doughnuts) are a nice touch. Refreshments may also be provided during the focus group session to add a degree of informality.

Recording the Focus Group

If the room in which you will be meeting is designed for focus groups, a tape recording system should be available. The microphone designed to carry the conversation into the observation room is also connected to a recorder. If this technology is available, make arrangements prior to the day of the focus group to test the system and be sure you know how to operate it.

If you do not have access to such a room, or if the room is not equipped with recording equipment, simply obtain a tape recorder and microphone and place it on the table around which the group is sitting.

Test the equipment, batteries, and microphone well before the meeting. Be sure that the microphone will pick up the comments when group members are seated around the table.

At the outset of the meeting, the group should be made aware that the session is being recorded to keep accurate and complete records of the group's comments and to allow the focus group leader to concentrate on the conversation rather than on taking notes. Permission to record the session should be asked of the participants. If anyone strongly objects, don't use it. Few, however, should have a problem with it.

Inviting Observers

If there are people in the church who you feel would benefit from or be interested in observing the focus group, you may wish to invite them. Often this can be an eye-opening experience for people who have difficulty believing that a new service is really needed. When these people hear comments from your target group, their paradigms are often shifted for a lifetime.

If you are not able to conduct the focus group in a room with a two-way mirror, several observers may sit in the room but should be physically removed from the discussion group. They should be introduced as observers. Participants should be encouraged to ignore them, and the observers should not participate in the inter-action of the focus group.

Questions for Focus Group Participants

1. Have you ever been a member of a church? If so, what were your experiences?
2. Do you have any impressions about church? What are they? (Include both positive and negative images you have of church.)
3. Do you know how you came to these opinions?
4. A commitment of this church is to provide need-meeting services to the members of this community. Is there any-thing you can think of that would be beneficial to you and your family and that you feel a church could provide?
5. Do you recall ever seeing any advertisement or general mail-ing from a church? If so, do you have any impressions of the church because of that advertisement?
6. Look at the following brochure. [Your church's publicity for the new service.] Please read it and give us your candid response.
7. If you were looking for a church home, what would be most important to you?
8. If you could give some advice to the leadership of this church, what would it be?

Appendix D

"Discover the Power of Healing Hope"

Rev. Joe Harding
(Sample Sermon)

The following sermon illustrates the principles discussed in chapter 7 on a well-prepared sermon.[1]

There was a man who made a terrifying discovery! He was shocked and stunned. At first he could not believe what he had seen. He knew it had happened to other people. He could not believe it could ever happen to him. The awful discovery kept him awake at night. When he did sleep, he would have alarming dreams and awaken in the darkness, choking with anxiety and dread. Again and again in the darkness, as his mind cleared, he would have to face the frightening reality. The nightmare was true. This terrible thing was actually happening to him! He could not imagine or pretend it away.

His wife noticed. His friends noticed. He looked haggard, worn and hollow-eyed.

He knew what he had to do. He had to make a journey. It was all so strange, so mysterious. He told them he would be gone a few days. His wife and children were not to worry. He would return. Everything would be all right.

The long, lonely journey began. The family waved good-bye. The man turned away; his eyes filled with tears. He walked alone, carrying in his heart the knowledge of the terrifying discovery.

Finally he reached the city. He went to a certain room which was part of a great building called the Temple. He met a man he had never seen before—a priest. The frightened man described the awful discovery; then he showed the priest the white spots on his legs and arms. The priest shook his head slowly. He had seen the spots before. He noticed that body hair on the spots was also white. He was careful not to touch the man.

The priest's eyes narrowed. His jaw was set. "I declare before God that you are now unclean. God's Word says, 'The leper who has the disease shall wear torn clothes and let the hair on his head hang loose, and he shall cover his upper lip and cry, "Unclean, unclean." He shall remain unclean as long as he has the disease; he shall dwell alone in a habitation outside the camp.' [Lev. 13:45–46 RSV] May God have mercy on you."

The priest left. The man stood alone. Stunned, tears streamed down his cheeks. His body crumpled. He sobbed.

He knew what it meant. He could no longer hold his children in his arms. He could no longer embrace his wife. He could no longer give or receive the handclasp of a friend. He could no longer worship in the synagogue nor earn his living at his trade. What would become of his wife and children? They would be left desolate!

Slowly he began to tear his clothes so they were like ragged shreds. Then he took his hand and messed his hair up until it was wild and unkempt. Shuffling, he stepped out into the street, his stooped shoulders sagging. He put his hand to his mouth, covered his upper lip, and cried, "Unclean! Unclean!" For the first time in his life he saw people afraid of him. They stepped back. They looked with disgust. Parents grabbed their children. "Unclean! Unclean!" His voice echoed through the streets. The way opened before him. He walked alone.

He approached his own village. He saw it in the distance. This would be the hardest part of all. His children would want to rush out to embrace him. His wife would want to kiss him, leprosy or not. He must be strong. He must protect them, even if it broke their hearts. Still, he must not allow them to touch him.

So the tragic scene unfolded. The father seemed to be very angry with his children. He told them to keep away. He told his wife to come no further. His appearance frightened them. He seemed like a snarling animal. Actually his heart was breaking. He turned back to his leper caves. They went back to their lonely home.

All this is by way of background for our text in the Gospel of Luke, which begins with the words, "While he was in one of the cities, there came a man full of leprosy . . ."

Focus with me upon that phrase "there came a man full of leprosy."

Full of Leprosy

I want to suggest, first of all, that the phrase gives us a clue to understanding ourselves and other people. "Full of leprosy," full of problems, of ugliness, of a loathsomeness which if revealed would repel people.

Now perhaps you want to say to me, "Joe, I am glad you are talking about this problem because I am sure there are a lot of people with the problem. But me? I'm fine. No problems. I don't feel like a leper. I feel just great."

This is the conscious mind or ego defending itself, maintaining its appearance of health. We know that there is much more to the self than the conscious or surface mind. Chances are that you have an inner leper roaming around in there in the dark caves, crying out, "Unclean! Unclean!" He or she is that poor, ragged, bedraggled, ugly shadow figure that we want kept alone "in a habitation outside the camp."

I also believe I am safe in saying that rather recently someone has addressed you like the priest in that little room. Someone has sent a message with burning, narrowed eyes and a judgmental set of the jaw. You could almost feel them backing away. "You are no good. You are a bad person. You are sick. You are terrible. You are a failure."

There is a devastating scene in the novel *The Cracker Factory* by Joyce Roberta-Burditt. Cassie, a woman who drinks too much and is hospitalized for emotional distress, is writing to her brother, Bob. This is part of what she writes:

> It's been one hell of a year. I've been running around half crazy, trying to remember whatever it is Alexander [her psychiatrist] said I learned in the hospital the last time. Bob, I don't even know. I just know that I'm coming unraveled and can't seem to stop it. It's been a whole year of Charles' [her husband] running off and slamming doors when I need him. I tell him I'm sick and he says, "You're telling me? I'm sick of your sickness." And . . . bam . . . out the door.
>
> He looked at me one night and said, "Cassie, you're a loser." Bob, when I stand on Judgment Day to hear myself condemned to hell, it will be no more devastating and irrevocable than Charlie's "you're a loser." Forever defective. Forever doomed. No hope at all.

That's modern leprosy. It happens all the time. It happens to children—to abused children, abandoned children, to handicapped children.

The Bible says, "There came a man full of leprosy . . ."

I want to share with you a story that first appeared in the *Journal of the National Education Association*. It is a poignant story called "Cipher in the Snow."

> It started with tragedy on a biting cold February morning. I was driving behind the Milford Corners' bus as I did on most snowy mornings on my way to school. It veered and stopped short at the hotel, which it had no business doing; and I was annoyed as I had to come to an unexpected stop. A boy lurched out of the bus, stumbled, and collapsed on the snow bank at the curb. The bus driver and I reached him at the same moment. His thin hollow face was white even against the snow.

"He's dead," the driver whispered. It didn't register for a minute. I glanced quickly at the scared young faces staring down at us from the school bus.

"Get a doctor! Quick!" I yelled.

"No use, I tell you, he's dead." The driver looked down at the boy's still form. "He never even said he felt bad," he muttered, "just tapped me on the shoulder and said, real quiet, 'I'm sorry. I have to get off at the hotel.' That's all. Polite and apologizing like."

At school, the giggling, shuffling morning noise quieted as the news went down the halls. I passed a huddle of girls. "Who was it? Who dropped dead on the way to school?" I heard one of the half whispers. "Don't know his name—some kid from Milford Corners," was the reply.

It was like that in the faculty room and the principal's office. "I'd appreciate your going out to tell the parents," the principal told me. "They haven't a phone, and anyway somebody from the school should go out there in person. I'll cover your classes."

"Why me?" I asked. "Wouldn't it be better if you did it?"

"I didn't know the boy," the principal admitted levelly. "And in last year's sophomore personalities column I note that you were listed as his favorite teacher."

I drove through the snow and cold, down the bad canyon road to the place and thought about the boy, Cliff Evans. His favorite teacher! I thought. He hasn't spoken two words to me in two years. I could see him in my mind's eye all right, sitting back there in the last seat in my room by himself and left by himself. "Cliff Evans," I muttered to myself, "a boy who never talked." I thought for a moment. "A boy who never smiled. I never saw him smile once."

The big ranch kitchen was clean and warm. I blurted out my news somehow. Mrs. Evans reached blindly toward a chair. "He never said anything about bein' ailing." His step-father snorted, "He ain't said nothing about anything since I moved in here."

After school I sat in the office and stared bleakly at the records spread out before me. I was to close the file and write the obituary for the school paper. The almost bare sheets mocked my effort. Cliff Evans, white, never legally adopted by the step-father, five younger half brothers and sisters. These meager strands of information and the list of "D" grades were all the records had to offer.

Cliff Evans had silently come in the school door in the mornings and gone out the school door in the evening, and that was all. He had never belonged to a club. He had never played on a team.

He had never held an office. As far as I could tell, he had never done one happy, noisy, kid thing. He had never been anybody at all.

How do you go about making a boy into a zero? The grade school records showed me. The first and second grade teacher's annotations read, "Sweet, shy child." "Timid, but eager." Then the third grade note had opened the attack. Some teacher had written in a good, firm hand, "Cliff won't talk. Uncooperative. Slow learner. The other academic sheets had followed with "dull;" "slow witted;" "I.Q.—low." They became correct. The boy's I.Q. score in the ninth grade was listed at 83. But his I.Q. in the third grade had been 106. The score didn't go under a hundred until the seventh grade. Even shy, timid, sweet children have resilience. It takes time to break them.

I wrote a brief, savage report, pointing out what education had done to Cliff Evans. I slapped a copy on the principal's desk and another in the sad, dog-eared file. I banged the typewriter and slammed the file drawer, but I didn't feel much better. A little boy had kept walking after me, a little boy with a peaked pale face; a skinny body in faded jeans and big eyes that had looked and searched for a long time and then had become veiled.

I could guess how many times he had been chosen last to play sides in a game, how many whispered child conversations had excluded him, how many times he hadn't been asked. I could see and hear the faces and voices that had said over and over again, "You're dumb. You're dumb! You're a nothing, Cliff Evans."

A child is a believing creature. Cliff undoubtedly believed them. Suddenly it seemed clear to me; when finally there was nothing left at all for Cliff Evans, he collapsed in a snow bank and went away. The doctor might list "heart failure" as the cause of death, but he wouldn't change my mind.

We couldn't find ten students in school who had known Cliff well enough to attend the funeral as his friends. So the student body officers and a committee from the Junior Class went as a group to the church, being politely sad. I attended the services with them and sat through it with a lump of cold lead in my chest and a big resolve growing through me.

I've never forgotten Cliff Evans, nor that resolve. He has been my challenge year after year, class after class. I look up and down the rows carefully each September at the unfamiliar faces. I look for veiled eyes or bodies scourged into a seat in an alien world.

"Look kids," I said to myself silently. "I may not do anything else for you this year, but not one of you is going to come out of here a nobody. I'll work or fight to the bitter end, doing battle with society or the school board or anybody else, but I won't have one of you coming out of here thinking himself into a zero."

Most of the time—not always, but most of the time, I've succeeded.

It seems to me that is what it means to be a follower of Jesus. It means to find and care about lepers.

Luke tells us, "There came a man full of leprosy." This man is a symbol of the pain, the loneliness, the disease, the despair that is out in that world. He is the prisoner in our state prison, he is the old man or woman in the nursing home, the mentally retarded child, the young prostitute downtown, the person who was used and abandoned last night. Full of leprosy, running over with hopelessness, weighted down with guilt.

Can anyone do anything to help the man, these people? Too often the church has followed the stern Jerusalem priest rather than Jesus. Too often the church has pointed its finger and said, "You are a leper. Get out!"

One afternoon in January, I stood shivering in the cold, looking through a tiny slit of a window into the chancel area in an English cathedral. My friend, a Welsh pastor, explained, "This is a leper's window. Leprosy was brought back by the crusaders during the Middle Ages. Lepers couldn't enter the church. They stood outside looking in." Newcomers can feel like lepers if the church doesn't want them. The relational coldness is as effective as that tiny window!

When He Saw Jesus

Notice with me the turning point in our story. Just a few words tell the story: "And when he saw Jesus . . ." When the people in Nazareth saw Jesus, they saw only a man, only the carpenter—Joseph's son, whom they had known for at least a quarter of a century. When the leper saw Jesus, he saw so much more. He saw someone who cared. He saw someone who could help. He

255

looked at Jesus and saw beyond his old problems to the new possibilities of a new creation, new health. He saw the impossibilities banished.

That is the picture that gave him such boldness as he ran forward and said, "Lord, if you will, you can make me clean." You can make me clean.

Now I have to ask myself at this point, How do I see Jesus, really? Do I see him as the remote and distant figure like a great faded painting in a church, or the object of years of theological and biblical studies? Have my years of knowledge about Jesus left me like the Nazareth neighbors? Do I assume I always know all there is to know about him? Have I confused him with the Jerusalem priest?

Is it possible that I, a professional clergyman, pastor of a great church, can find healing for my needs? Can I see in the face of Jesus one who cares about me?

"Lord, if you will, you can make me clean."

We read on: "And he stretched out his hand, and touched him, saying, 'I will; be clean.'"

I can't overestimate the importance of that touch. You see, everyone knew the contaminating power of leprosy. If you touched a leper, you were unclean. You were contaminated by the touch. Parents told their children, "Whatever you do, don't touch a leper. Don't let one touch you."

Now Jesus reaches out. He touches a leper. Here is a struggle. Which power is greater? Which force is stronger? Will Jesus become a leper? Or will the leper be healed?

This is why our text has such a shot of victory. It is Jesus Christ who speaks. Leprosy has been saying, "Be sick; be lonely; be forsaken; be discouraged." Now there is a greater voice, Be clean. "And immediately the leprosy left him." It got shoved out, replaced by a greater power—the healing, saving love of God.

Now the sequel to the story sounds strange to our ears. Stay with me for a few more minutes. "And he charged him to tell no one; but 'go and show yourself to the priest, and make an offering for your cleansing, as Moses commanded, for a proof to the people.'"

Jesus tells the man to follow the Law in claiming the healing. His excited witness is to be withheld until his healing is verified by the priest and the gratitude offering for healing is made.

Watch this man with me as he hurries to Jerusalem. We saw his first journey of sadness and despair. Now see his journey of joy and victory. He sings. He runs. He shouts praises to God. The sky is blue. The flowers are beautiful. He smiles and greets people. He still has on those old leper clothes. He still scares some people. But he knows he is no longer a leper!

He can't wait for the priest to come and examine him. "Well, what do you think? Am I cured?" The priest is silent. He calls in another priest. They look at his arms, legs, chest, neck, head, abdomen. They have a whole committee looking for leprosy, and they can't find it!

The man tells them about Jesus, and the priest tells him there must have been a mistaken diagnosis in the first place.

The ritual of cleansing is very interesting. Let's watch it together. (You can read this in Leviticus 14.) The man brings two birds as a sacrifice. One bird is killed; its blood is taken and sprinkled over the man as the priest dips hyssop in the blood and sprinkles him from head to toe, seven times! The other bird is set free! Then the man washes his clothes, bathes, and shaves his head, his beard, his eyebrows. He has to wait eight days.

On the eighth day, they take a lamb and kill it as a guilt offering. The priest takes the blood of the lamb and he touches the right ear of the man, the right thumb, and the big toe of his right foot.

Then he takes oil and sprinkles it seven times on the man—touches his right ear, right thumb, right toe with the oil and pours the rest of the oil over his head. Then the priest says, "Go. You are clean."

Now the man rushes home. Word has gone before him. Here he comes, scrubbed, shaved, cleansed, healed. A little dried blood is still on his ear, his thumb, his toe. His shaved head with the oil still there looks like a peeled onion, glistening in the afternoon sun.

We know the Aramaic word those children spoke. We know the word they cried in joy! "Abba! Abba!"—which means "Daddy! Daddy!" He swept them into his arms. He kissed his wife. He danced and sang. And he told them the story of the man who had healed him.

He didn't know that Jesus would one day die on the cross to bring healing to all who would accept and receive it. He didn't know Jesus would pour out the Holy Spirit like anointing oil to make us King's children. He *did* know that once he was a leper. Now he was healed.

The man couldn't quit talking about Jesus. Luke says, "So much the more the report went abroad concerning Jesus; and great multitudes gathered to hear and to be healed of their infirmities."

Appendix E

How Was Our Service?

(Evaluation Form)

Use or adapt this evaluation form to (1) evaluate other churches in your area that you visit in your research, and (2) allow guests who visit to evaluate your new service.

259

Facility

Ease in Finding Location

1 2 3 4 5 6 7
Poor   Acceptable   Excellent
Comments

First Impression of Outside

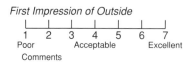

1 2 3 4 5 6 7
Poor   Acceptable   Excellent
Comments

First Impression of Inside
(upon immediately entering)

1 2 3 4 5 6 7
Poor   Acceptable   Excellent
Comments

Impression of Inside
(after the service)

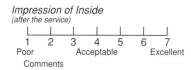

1 2 3 4 5 6 7
Poor   Acceptable   Excellent
Comments

Parking

Adequacy of Spaces

1 2 3 4 5 6 7
Poor   Acceptable   Excellent
Comments

Proximity to Entrance

1 2 3 4 5 6 7
Poor   Acceptable   Excellent
Comments

Nursery

First Impression Upon Entering

1 2 3 4 5 6 7
Poor   Acceptable   Excellent
Comments

*Confidence in Nursery Staff
and Operations*

1 2 3 4 5 6 7
Poor   Acceptable   Excellent
Comments

Impression Upon Leaving Nursery

1 2 3 4 5 6 7
Poor   Acceptable   Excellent
Comments

Signs

*Directions from Parking Area
to Appropriate Building Entrance*

1 2 3 4 5 6 7
Poor   Acceptable   Excellent
Comments

Where to Get General Information

1 2 3 4 5 6 7
Poor   Acceptable   Excellent
Comments

Directions to Sanctuary/Worship Center

1 2 3 4 5 6 7
Poor   Acceptable   Excellent
Comments

Signs *continued*

Directions to Restrooms

1   2   3   4   5   6   7
Poor   Acceptable   Excellent

Comments

Directions to Nursery

1   2   3   4   5   6   7
Poor   Acceptable   Excellent

Comments

What other information or directions did you desire?

Sanctuary

First Impression Upon Entering Sanctuary/Worship Center

1   2   3   4   5   6   7
Poor   Acceptable   Excellent

Comments

Visibility

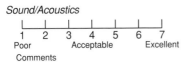

1   2   3   4   5   6   7
Poor   Acceptable   Excellent

Comments

Sound/Acoustics

1   2   3   4   5   6   7
Poor   Acceptable   Excellent

Comments

Ease in Being Seated

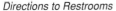

1   2   3   4   5   6   7
Poor   Acceptable   Excellent

Comments

Rest Rooms

First Impression Upon Entering

1   2   3   4   5   6   7
Poor   Acceptable   Excellent

Comments

Education Classrooms

First Impression Upon Entering

1   2   3   4   5   6   7
Poor   Acceptable   Excellent

Comments

Worship Service

Music

1   2   3   4   5   6   7
Poor   Acceptable   Excellent

Comments

Welcome to Visitors

1   2   3   4   5   6   7
Poor   Acceptable   Excellent

Comments

Theme

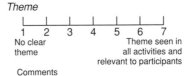

1   2   3   4   5   6   7
No clear   Theme seen in
theme   all activities and
                            relevant to participants

Comments

Worship Service *continued*

Bulletin/Program

```
1   2   3   4   5   6   7
```
Like the classified ads   Attractive,
                                     well prepared

Comments

Announcements

```
1   2   3   4   5   6   7
```
A distraction   Blends into service

Comments

Response

```
1   2   3   4   5   6   7
```
No opportunity   Appropriate
to respond to the   opportunity
message   to respond

Comments

Flow

```
1   2   3   4   5   6   7
```
Various components   Each component
are disjointed   is part of the whole
                            and fits together

Comments

Language

```
1   2   3   4   5   6   7
```
Archaic with mostly   Clear communication
religious jargon   widely understood

Comments

Notes

Introduction

1. "Pastoral Tenure and Church Growth," *The Win Arn Growth Report* 25: 2.

2. If you think your church is not ready for a new service but does need to change, feel free to write me for recommendations. At the time of this publishing, my address is: P.O. Box 541, Monrovia, CA 91107.

3. For helpful information on current architectural implications on church growth see Ray Bowman, *When Not to Build* (Grand Rapids: Baker, 1994).

4. Carl George, *How to Break Growth Barriers* (Grand Rapids: Baker, 1993), 178.

5. Lyle Schaller, *Forty-Four Ways to Increase Church Attendance* (Nashville: Abingdon Press, 1988), 102.

Chapter 1: *Why Start a New Service?*

1. Arnell ArnTessoni (lecture, Greenlake, Wis., April 1993).

2. Win Arn and Charles Arn, *The Master's Plan for Making Disciples* (Monrovia, Calif.: Church Growth Press, 1982), 43.

3. "Do You Know Your 'Potential Congregation'?" *The Win Arn Growth Report* 18: 3.

4. Schaller, *Forty-Four Ways to Increase Church Attendance,* 50.

5. James White, *Opening the Front Door: Worship and Church Growth* (Nashville: Convention Press, 1992), 29.

6. Aubrey Malphurs, *Pouring New Wine into Old Wineskins* (Grand Rapids: Baker, 1993), 161–62.

7. "Is Your Church in a Mid-Life Crisis?" *The Win Arn Growth Report* 7: 2.

8. *Shaping a Future for the Church in the Changing Community* (Atlanta: Home Mission Board, Southern Baptist Convention, 1984).

9. Charles Arn, "How Do You Begin a New Lifecycle?" *The Win Arn Growth Report* 21: 3.

10. *Lifeline* newsletter 12 (Arcadia, Calif.: LIFE International, 1994): 3.

Chapter 2: *The Role of the Pastor*

1. Donald M. Brandt, *Worship and Outreach: New Services for New People* (Minneapolis: Augsburg, 1994), 10.

263

2. Spiritual gifts definitions taken from Peter Wagner, *Your Spiritual Gifts Can Help Your Church Grow* (Ventura, Calif.: Regal, 1979, 1994), 253–58.

3. See such books as Aubrey Malphurs, *Developing a Vision for Ministry* (Grand Rapids: Baker, 1992); George Barna, *The Power of Vision* (Ventura, Calif.: Regal, 1992); Truman Brown, *Visionary Leadership for Churches* (Nashville: Convention Press, 1991); Robert Dale, *Keeping the Dream Alive* (Nashville: Broadman, 1988); Robert Dale, *To Dream Again* (Nashville: Broadman, 1981).

4. Robert Greenleaf, "What Is Your Dream?" *The Win Arn Growth Report* 8: 2.

5. George, *How to Break Growth Barriers,* 178.

6. Letter from Rev. Hylyard Irvin, Glendale First Church of the Nazarene, Glendale, Ariz., to Rev. Ted Underwood, Bakersfield Church of the Nazarene (November 20, 1992).

7. Donald McGavran and Win Arn, *How to Grow a Church* (16mm film) (Monrovia, Calif.: Church Growth, Inc., 1973).

8. Robert Thomas, "Personality Characteristics of Effective Revitalization Pastors in Small, Passive Baptist General Conference Churches" (Ph.D. diss., Talbot Theological Seminary, 1989), 102.

9. Malphurs, *Pouring New Wine into Old Wineskins,* 70.

10. *The Win Arn Growth Report* 36: 3.

11. Wilbur Brannon, *Multiple Services: A Strategy for Growth* (Kansas City: Division of Church Growth, Church of the Nazarene, 1992), 32–33.

12. Elmer Towns, *How to Go to Two Services* (Lynchburg, Va.: Church Growth Institute, 1991), 9.

13. Malphurs, *Pouring New Wine into Old Wineskins,* 79–97.

14. George Barna, *What Americans Believe* (Ventura, Calif.: Regal, 1991), 185.

15. Leith Anderson, *Dying for Change* (Minneapolis: Bethany, 1990).

16. See Malphurs, *Pouring New Wine into Old Wineskins;* Lyle Schaller, *Strategies for Change* (Nashville: Abingdon Press, 1993); Anderson, *Dying for Change.*

17. Ed Dobson, *Starting a Seeker-Sensitive Service* (Grand Rapids: Zondervan, 1993), 97.

18. Brannon, *Multiple Services: A Strategy for Growth,* 27.

19. See *The Growth Timer* (Kansas City: Division of Church Growth, Church of the Nazarene, 1989).

20. Charles Laird (correspondence with author, December 15, 1995).

Chapter 3: *Getting the Church on Board*

1. Paul Mundey, *Change and the Established Congregation* (Elgin, Ill.: The Andrew Center, 1994), 33.

2. George, *How to Break Growth Barriers,* 178.

3. *Questions and Answers Concerning Multiple Worship Service Options* (Pasadena, Calif.: First Nazarene Church, 1993).

4. Robert Logan, *Beyond Church Growth* (Old Tappan, N.J.: Revell, 1989), 64.

5. Mundey, *Change and the Established Congregation,* 36.

6. Malphurs, *Pouring New Wine into Old Wineskins,* 80.

7. Dobson, *Starting a Seeker-Sensitive Service,* 24.

8. For a helpful book on managing disagreement in the church, see Speed Leas, *Managing Conflict in the Church* (Nashville: Abingdon Press, 1973).

9. *A Church for the Twenty-First Century* video is available for $29.95 from Church Growth, Inc., P.O. Box 541, Monrovia, CA 91017 or call 626-305-1280. This excellent video can be a helpful ally in introducing the idea of a new service.

10. Malphurs, *Pouring New Wine into Old Wineskins*, 104.

11. Doug Murren, "The Process of Change," *Worship Leader* (September/October 1995): 30.

12. Anderson, *Dying for Change*, 177–78.

13. Lyle Schaller, "How Do You Count?" *Church Growth: America* 5, no. 4, 9.

14. Win Arn, *The Church Growth Ratio Book* (Monrovia, Calif.: Church Growth Press, 1990), 47.

15. The Shawnee Park Christian Reformed Church (Grand Rapids, Mich.) is one example of a church governing body that appointed an ad hoc committee to investigate and make a recommendation on the feasibility of conducting an alternative worship service. The committee's ten-page report addressed eight questions: (1) Why an alternative service? (2) Who is to be reached? (3) What type of alternative service? (4) How would the service be implemented? (5) When could it begin? (6) How would it begin? (7) How much money would it cost? (8) What would be the expected impact on existing ministries? This outline presents a good organizational tool for an exploratory committee.

16. Lyle Schaller, "One Worship Service or Two?" *The Parish Paper* 9, no. 8 (February 1980), 1.

17. Ibid., 2.

18. Brandt, *Worship and Outreach*, 35.

19. Doug Samples, "Questions Regarding Multiple Services" (internal document circulated among Bakersfield First Church of the Nazarene leadership).

20. Steve Green (congregational letter dated July 13, 1993, Pasadena First Church of the Nazarene).

21. Mundey, *Change and the Established Congregation*, 36.

Chapter 4: *What Kind of Service Do You Want?*

1. There are early indications that a fourth generational group may be emerging in the American sociodemographic landscape: middle adults. These are people between the ages of fifty and seventy. They are distinct from Baby Boomers but also are not senior adults. For more information see Win Arn, "Middle Adults: A New Approach to Older Adult Ministry," *LifeLine* newsletter 18. Available from LIFE Int'l., 1857 Highland Oaks Dr., Arcadia, CA 91006.

2. *LifeLine* 18: 1.

3. Ken Dychtwald, *Age Wave* (New York: Bantam, 1990), 6.

4. Arnell Motz, *Reclaiming a Nation* (Winnipeg: Trinity Western Press, 1990), 163.

5. David Gergen, "Sixty-Something," *U.S. News & World Report* (April 16, 1990), 64.

6. Win Arn, "Redefining Senior Adults," *The New Senior* (Arcadia, Calif.: LIFE Int'l., 1993), 3.

7. Landon Y. Jones, *Great Expectations: America and the Baby Boom Generation* (New York: Ballantine, 1980), 1.

8. Bob Bast, *The Missing Generation* (Monrovia, Calif.: Church Growth Press, 1991), 57–61.

9. Gary McIntosh, *Three Generations* (Grand Rapids: Revell, 1995), 139–43.

10. Ibid., 185–86.

11. Jack Hayford, John Killinger, and Howard Stevenson, *Mastering Worship* (Portland: Multnomah, 1990), 26.

12. Ibid., 126–27.

13. George Hunter, *Church for the Unchurched* (Nashville: Abingdon Press, 1996), 55.

14. Rick Warren, "Finding Ethnic America," *The Purpose-Driven Church* (Grand Rapids: Zondervan, 1995), 253–54.

15. Ted Yamamori, *The Pastor's Church Growth Handbook,* ed. Win Arn (Monrovia, Calif.: Church Growth Press, 1984), 171.

16. Brandt, *Worship and Outreach,* 12.

17. Donald McGavran and Win Arn, *How to Grow a Church* (Ventura, Calif.: Regal, 1973), 44.

18. See Joel Garreau, *Nine Nations of North America* (Boston: Houghton Mifflin, 1981).

19. Sally Morgenthaller, "Worship Evangelism: Bringing Down the Walls," *Evangelism* 8, no. 2 (February 1994): 53.

20. Brandt, *Worship and Outreach,* 8: 20.

21. *A Church for the 21st Century* (Monrovia, Calif.: Church Growth, Inc., 1994).

Chapter 5: *What Kind of Service Do They Want?*

1. Brandt, *Worship and Outreach,* 12.

2. "Listening to the Unchurched," *Netfax* 25 (August 7, 1995): 1.

3. Deborah Bell, lay elder (personal letter, July 21, 1993).

4. Adapted from "Taking the Pulse of Your Community," *The Win Arn Growth Report* 35: 4.

5. "Listening to the Unchurched," 1.

6. Anderson, *Dying for Change,* 99.

7. Warren, *The Purpose-Driven Church,* 169–71.

Chapter 6: *When and Where to Meet*

1. Gary McIntosh, "Multiple Worship Services," *The Church Growth Network* 5, no. 4: 1.

2. "Multiple Worship Services," *The Church Growth Network* 5, no. 5: 1.

3. Schaller, *Forty-Four Ways to Increase Church Attendance,* 62.

4. Lyle Schaller, "One Worship Service or Two?" *The Parish Paper* 9, no. 8: 1.

5. Schaller, *Forty-Four Ways to Increase Church Attendance,* 62.

6. Heather Wolfe, "Double Your Pleasure," *Net Results* (March 1995): 6.

7. David Schieber, "How Presbyterian Churches Can Reach Baby Boomers" (lecture, Memphis, Tenn., January 24, 1993).

8. Elmer Towns, "Multiple Services," *The Christian Times Today* 1 (January 1995): 3.

9. Josh Hunt, "Saturday Night's All Right for Worship," *Growing Churches* (July/August/September 1994): 22.

10. Mundey, *Change and the Established Congregation,* 3.

11. Doug Murren, "Adding Services," *Boomerang Fax* (May 5, 1993): 1.

12. Charles Arn, *Growth: A New Vision for the Sunday School* (Monrovia, Calif.: Church Growth Press, 1984).

13. "Close Down Your Children's Sunday School," *The Win Arn Growth Report* 34: 1, 4.

14. "Stop That Building Committee," *The Win Arn Growth Report* 39: 4.

15. Bowman, *When Not to Build* (Grand Rapids: Baker, 1994).

16. William P. Wood, "Your Church Building Program: Facing the Risks," *Church Growth: America* 8, no. 3: 4.

17. Bob E. Logan and Steven L. Ogne, "The Church Planter's Toolkit," (Wheaton: CRM Church Mart, 1992).

18. Arnell Arn, *Church Parenting for the Twenty-First Century* video (Valley Forge, Pa.: Division of National Ministries, 1995).

19. Schaller, *Forty-Four Ways to Increase Church Attendance,* 73.

20. Ray Bowman (conversation, June 11, 1996).

21. Schaller, *Forty-Four Ways to Increase Church Attendance,* 92ff.

22. Flavil Yeakley, *Why Churches Grow* (Arvada, Colo.: Christian Communication, 1979), 89.

23. McIntosh, "Multiple Worship Services," 1.

24. See Kennon Callahan, *Twelve Keys to an Effective Church* (New York: Harper, 1993), chap. 3, for more helpful discussion on seating capacity.

25. Robert A. Lee, "Transformations to Nontraditional Church Structures," *Net Results* (August 1992): 8.

26. James F. White, *A Brief History of Christian Worship* (Nashville: Abingdon Press, 1993), 170.

27. Towns, *How to Go to Two Services,* 20.

28. Ibid., 23.

29. McIntosh, "Multiple Worship Services," 1.

Chapter 7: *Designing the Service*

1. Paul Anderson, "Balancing Tradition and Innovation," *Word and Worship,* vol. 1 of *Leadership Handbooks of Practical Theology,* ed. James Berkley (Grand Rapids: Baker, 1992).

2. Bob Bast, *Attracting New Members* (Monrovia, Calif.: Church Growth Press, 1988), 67–68.

3. Schaller, *Forty-Four Ways to Increase Church Attendance,* 23.

4. J. Howard Griffith, "Membership Growth Insights from a Sabbatical," *Net Results* (October 1994): 14.

5. Pete Ward, *Worship and Youth Culture* (London: Marshall Pickering, 1993), 14–15.

6. Steve Sjogren, "Worship Sensitivity," *Equipping the Saints* (January/February/March 1995): 23.

7. Warren, *The Purpose-Driven Church,* 280.

8. George Hunter, *How to Reach Secular People* (Nashville: Abingdon Press, 1992), 68.

9. Dori E. Collins, "Lutheran Worship in the Nineties Sound," *Perspectives* 5 (March 1993): 17.

10. Lyle Schaller, "Schaller on Contemporary Worship," *Worship Leader* (July/August, 1995): 35.

11. Paul Anderson, "Drama in Church," *Word and Worship,* vol. 1 of *Leadership Handbooks of Practical Theology,* 253.

12. Ibid.

13. More information is available by calling: 615-251-3837.

14. More information is available by calling: 800-876-7335.

15. More information is available by calling: 800-877-0700.

16. Thomas Boomershire, *Story Telling* (Nashville: Abingdon Press, 1988), 18.

17. A helpful book, from a Christian perspective, is William R. White, *Stories for the Journey: A Sourcebook for Christian Story Tellers* (Minneapolis: Augsburg, 1988).

18. For free information write to: NAPPS, P.O. Box 309, Jonesborough, TN 37659.

19. Jim Tippens, "Puppetry: It's Not Just for Kids Anymore," *Worship Leader* (January/February 1995): 12.

20. Brandt, *Worship and Outreach*, 28.

21. Karen Mains, "Symbolism in Worship," *Word and Worship*, vol. 1 of *Leadership Handbooks of Practical Theology*, 249.

22. Griffith, "Membership Growth Insights from a Sabbatical," 9.

23. Ward, *Worship and Youth Culture*, 154–55.

24. Joe Harding, *Have I Told You Lately?* (Monrovia, Calif.: Church Growth Press, 1982), 31–35.

25. Warren, *The Purpose-Driven Church*, 256.

26. Schaller, *Forty-Four Ways to Increase Church Attendance*, 33.

27. Kurt Frederickson in *A Church for the Twenty-First Century* (video).

Chapter 8: *Getting People to Come*

1. Win Arn and Charles Arn, *The Master's Plan for Making Disciples* (Monrovia, Calif.: Church Growth Press, 1982).

2. Win Arn, "Applying the 4Ps of Marketing," *The Win Arn Growth Report* 34: 3.

3. Flavil Yeakley, "A Profile of the New Convert: Change in Lifestyle Situation," *The Pastor's Church Growth Handbook,* ed. Win Arn (Monrovia, Calif.: Church Growth Press, 1982), 31–36.

4. Arn, "Applying the 4Ps of Marketing," 3.

5. Win Arn, "Who Found It?" *Church Growth: America* (Sept./Oct. 1978): 4.

6. Lyle Schaller, "Media and Church Growth," *Church Growth: America* 8, no. 2: 7.

7. See Walter Mueller, *Direct Mail Ministry* (Nashville: Abingdon Press, 1991).

8. Hunt, "Saturday Night's All Right for Worship," 23.

9. *Calling in Love* is a handbook for telephone outreach and is available for $29.95 from Church Growth, Inc. (P.O. Box 541, Monrovia, CA 91017) or call 626-305-1280.

10. Church Ad Project, 1021 Diffley Road, Eagan, MN 55123.

11. See Wayne Kiser, *Promotion Strategies for the Local Church* (Nashville: Broadman, 1992).

12. Doug Murren, "Adding Services," *Boomerang Fax* (May 5, 1993): 1.

13. "Ten Keys to Starting a Saturday Night Service," *Netfax* 29 (October 2, 1995): 1.

Chapter 9: *Evaluating the Service*

1. Letter from Rev. Hylyard Irvin to Rev. Doug Samples, Bakersfield First Church of the Nazarene, (November 1994).

2. McGavran and Arn, *How to Grow a Church* (16mm film).

3. Schaller, *Forty-Four Ways to Increase Church Attendance*, 53.

4. Ibid., 27.

Chapter 10: *Getting People to Come Back*

1. Arn, *The Church Growth Ratio Book*, 50.

2. Warren Hartman, *Membership Trends: A Study of Decline and Growth in the United Methodist Church* (Nashville: Discipleship Resources, 1980), 41.

3. Bast, *Attracting New Members*, 89–90.

4. "What Are First-Time Visitors Looking For?" *The Win Arn Growth Report* 24: 3.

5. Statistics compiled from Arn, *The Church Growth Ratio Book*, 47–51.

6. Charles Arn, "Decision-Making vs. Disciple-Making," *Church Growth: State of the Art*, ed. Peter Wagner (Wheaton, Ill.: Tyndale House, 1988), 145.

7. Win Arn, *The Pastor's Church Growth Handbook* (Monrovia, Calif.: Church Growth, Inc., 1992), 10.

8. Ibid., 43.

9. Arn, *The Church Growth Ratio Book*, 25–32.

10. Jeanne Hipp, *How to Start and Grow Small Groups* (Monrovia, Calif.: Church Growth Press, 1993). Available from Church Growth, Inc. (626-305-1280).

Appendix D: *"Discover the Power of Healing Hope"*

1. Text of this appendix is taken from Joe Harding, *Have I Told You Lately?* (Monrovia, Calif.: Church Growth Press, 1982), 65–75.

Dr. Charles Arn, a widely respected authority in the field of congregational growth strategy, is president of Church Growth, Inc., a research, development, and consulting organization specializing in congregational ministry and growth. Additional information on services is available from:

Church Growth, Inc.
P.O. Box 541
Monrovia, CA 91017

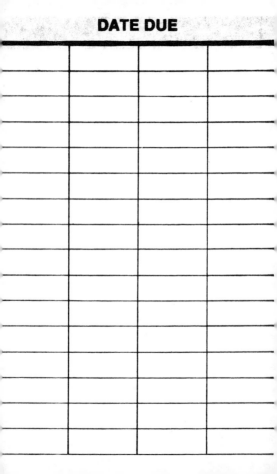

DATE DUE